Technological Challenges and Management

MATCHING HUMAN AND BUSINESS NEEDS

Manufacturing Design and Technology Series

Series Editor
J. Paulo Davim

PUBLISHED

Drills: Science and Technology of Advanced Operations
Viktor P. Astakhov

FORTHCOMING

Technological Challenges and Management: Matching Human and Business Needs
Feliciana Machado and Paulo Davim

Technological Challenges and Management

MATCHING HUMAN AND BUSINESS NEEDS

EDITED BY

CAROLINA MACHADO • J. PAULO DAVIM

CRC Press
Taylor & Francis Group
Boca Raton London New York

CRC Press is an imprint of the
Taylor & Francis Group, an **informa** business

CRC Press
Taylor & Francis Group
6000 Broken Sound Parkway NW, Suite 300
Boca Raton, FL 33487-2742

First issued in paperback 2020

ISBN-13: 978-1-4822-6101-1 (hbk)
ISBN-13: 978-0-367-78321-1 (pbk)

Visit the Taylor & Francis Web site at
http://www.taylorandfrancis.com

and the CRC Press Web site at
http://www.crcpress.com

Contents

Preface

Technological Challenges and Management: Matching Human and Business Needs is dedicated to technological challenges and management with special emphasis on the new advances and challenges that today's organizations face in the areas of human resources and business, resulting from continuous and highly complex changes in technological resources.

Nowadays, organizations face many challenges, namely, in the technological field, which causes many changes related to organizational structure and strategy. As a result, organizations need to implement a more proactive and flexible management, matching their human and business needs. Due to this reality, it is important to study and understand varied contributions made by researchers, academics, and practitioners in this field of study worldwide.

With the focus on this reality, this book aims to exchange experiences and perspectives about the state of technological challenges, management research, and future directions for this field of study, taking into account the deep implications that these challenges have in the organization of human resources. It aims to support academics and researchers and those operating in the management field in dealing with different challenges that organizations face today, with special emphasis on the relationship between technological changes, human resources management, and business.

For the purpose of sharing knowledge, through debate and information exchange, about technological challenges and management, and matching two critical items like human and business needs, this book is divided into seven chapters: Chapter 1 covers "Fashion or Adoption? Harmonization of New Technologies with Strategy, Structure, and Culture." Chapter 2 discusses "Technological and Organizational Changes: Challenges for HRM." Chapter 3 contains information on "The Concept of E-HRM, Its Evolution and Effects on Organizational Outcomes." Chapter 4 describes "Organizational Change Success as a Communicational Agency Effect: Structuration, Textualizing, and Networking." Subsequently,

Chapter 5 covers "E-HRM in SME: An Exploratory Study in a Portuguese Municipality." Chapter 6 describes "Collaboration in Processes Supported by Web 2.0: The Emergency of Interactivity." Finally, in Chapter 7 "Enhancing Online Fashion Retail: The Quest for the Perfect Fit" is presented.

We consider this as an excellent opportunity to participate in an exchange of information, ideas, and opinions about technological challenges and management and can say that this book is designed to increase the knowledge and understanding of all those involved in this field, in all kinds of organizations and activity sectors, such as human resource managers, managers in other areas, engineers, entrepreneurs, strategists, practitioners, academics, and researchers.

We are grateful to CRC Press/Taylor & Francis Group for this opportunity and for their professional support. Finally, we thank all chapter contributors for their interest and time allotted to work on this project.

Carolina Machado
Braga, Portugal

J. Paulo Davim
Aveiro, Portugal

Editors

Carolina Machado received her PhD in management sciences (organizational and politics management/human resources management) from the University of Minho, Braga, Portugal, in 1999, and a master's degree in management (strategic human resource management) from the Technical University of Lisbon, Lisbon, Portugal, in 1994. She has been teaching human resources management subjects since 1989 at the University of Minho and became an associate professor in 2004, with experience and research interest in the areas of human resource management, international human resource management, human resource management in small and medium-sized enterprises, training and development, and management change and knowledge management. Dr. Machado is the head of Human Resources Management Work Group at the University of Minho and the chief editor of the *International Journal of Applied Management Sciences and Engineering* (*IJAMSE*).

Institutional web page: http://www.eeg.uminho.pt; http://www.globalhrm.org.

J. Paulo Davim received his PhD in mechanical engineering from the University of Porto, Porto, Portugal, in 1997; the aggregate title from the University of Coimbra, Coimbra, Portugal, in 2005; and a DSc from London Metropolitan University, London, United Kingdom, in 2013. He is professor in the Department of Mechanical Engineering at the University of Aveiro, Aveiro, Portugal. He has more than 29 years of teaching and research experience in manufacturing and materials and mechanical engineering with special emphasis on machining and tribology. Recently, he became interested in management/industrial engineering and higher education for sustainability. Dr. Davim is the editor-in-chief of eight international journals, a guest editor of journals, a book editor, a book series editor, and a scientific advisory for many international journals and conferences. Presently, he is an editorial board member of 25 international journals and acts as a reviewer for more than 80 prestigious

ISI's Web of Science journals. In addition, he has also authored or coauthored more than 6 books, 50 book chapters, and 350 articles in journals and conferences (with more than 200 journal articles indexed in Web of Science: h-index 33+).

Personal web page: http://machining.web.ua.pt/pers-davim.htm.

Contributors

Catarina Rosa e Silva de Albuquerque
Faculty Damas
Recife, Brazil

Mouhannad Al-Sayegh
London College of Fashion
University of the Arts London
London, United Kingdom

Sara Carvalho
Department of Management
School of Economics and
    Management
University of Minho
Braga, Portugal

Jorge da Silva Correia-Neto
Department of Education
University Federal Rural of
    Pernambuco
Recife, Brazil

Ivo Manuel Pontes Domingues
Social Sciences Institute
University of Minho
Braga, Portugal

Jairo Simião Dornelas
Economic School
University Federal Rural of
    Pernambuco
Recife, Brazil

Mine Afacan Findikli
Faculty of Economic and
    administrative Sciences
Istanbul Gelisim University
Istanbul, Turkey

Susan Hamilton
London College of Fashion
University of the Arts London
London, United Kingdom

Carolina Machado
Department of Management
School of Economics and
    Management
University of Minho
Braga, Portugal

Maria Amélia Marques
Superior School of Business
    Sciences
Polytechnic Institute of Setúbal
Setúbal, Portugal

Fanke Peng
Media Arts and Digital Design
University of Canberra
Canberra, Australian Capital
    Territory, Australia

Yasin Rofcanin
Warwick Business School
University of Warwick
Coventry, United Kingdom
and
Faculty of Economic and
    Administrative Sciences
Istanbul Gelisim University
Istanbul, Turkey

**José Manuel Gameiro Rebelo
dos Santos**
Superior School of Business
    Sciences
Polytechnic Institute of Setúbal
Setúbal, Portugal

Yasemin Sen
School of Business
Istanbul University
Istanbul, Turkey

Alessandra Vecchi
London College of Fashion
University of the Arts London
London, United Kingdom

chapter one

Fashion or adoption? Harmonization of new technologies with strategy, structure, and culture

Yasemin Sen

Contents

Abstract

Advancements in the technological environment of businesses have forced organizations to keep up with rapid changes in order to not fall behind competitors. For this reason, organizations are in a race for the adoption of new technologies. But the following question remains: Are these organizations really ready for this technological advancement or is this new technology appropriate for these organizations? Therefore, this chapter aims to address the technology adoption issue and presents an insight into the alignment of new technology with the strategy, structure, and culture of an organization.

Keywords: Technology adoption, technology integration, culture, strategy, structure

1.1   Introduction

Organizations are not performing in a vacuum. They are surrounded by several environments and faced with different actors internally and externally. These actors can be customers, competitors, regulatory agencies, and suppliers, as well as employees or management. The main objective of any business is supporting its bottom line and maintaining its life in the long run. In order to achieve these aims, organizations need to satisfy customer needs and compete with other organizations by managing their operations. In business history, it is seen that competition has evolved in time. While initially the main concern of businesses was productivity, later on it became competition based on quality. However, today quality is also not sufficient to compete in the market. Providing better-quality products and services faster than other businesses and also considering sustainable development have become important issues for survival, including monitoring environmental changes very carefully and taking necessary actions.

Technological developments are also among the important changes that should be taken into consideration. As a result of the information age, the technological environment is one where rapid changes take place. Here, new solutions are continuously introduced, developed, and adopted by businesses. While some businesses implement new technologies as they are introduced, some adopt them from early adopter businesses (Butler & Sellbom, 2002:23). Many of these new technology adoptions do not bring expected results or end up with failures. The main reason behind these failures is the fact that new technologies are not standard prescriptions for all organizations. They should serve the purposes of organizations and should not be acquired just because they are popular. Each business has its own organizational context, namely, its own culture, structure, and strategy. When adopting a new technology, organizations should consider the issue of integration and make necessary adjustments. In the following sections, this issue will be discussed in detail.

1.2   "Technology" concept

More generally, the term "technology" means things that support organizational processes for maintaining business operations. This can be at the operational or knowledge level. Therefore, technology can be classified differently in this vein. *Operational technology* is defined as "equipping and sequencing of activities in the work flow which means producing and distributing output." But this work flow does not need to occur only in the factory. It can be a logistic activity for transferring a product to the marketplace and can be related with the manufacturing process of a physical product in the factory. On the other hand, *knowledge technology* is defined as "characteristics of knowledge used in the workflow" (Hickson, Pugh, & Pheysey, 1969:380). It can be the way of working, as well as the mental methods or information of techniques used in the production process (Kocel, 2005:273). Besides this general classification, there are also different classifications of technology in the literature. One of these categorizations can be seen in the study of Woodward. Woodward has investigated technology based on the technical complexity of the manufacturing process and proposed three types of technologies, namely, unit or small-batch production technology, large-batch or mass production technology, and continuous flow or process production technology (Blau, Falbe, McKinley, & Tracy, 1976:280). *Unit or small-batch production technology* refers to manufacturing individual or small-batch products based on the customer specifications stated in the order. Souvenir products that are specially produced for a name can be an example of this technology. *Large-batch or mass production technology* refers to manufacturing in large amounts in response to the continuous consumer demands in the industry. Production of white goods or cars can be examples of this category. Moreover, *continuous flow or process production technology* refers to "manufacturing of products measured and sold by weight, capacity or volume." The production of petroleum, natural gas, or chemicals are examples of this category (Tompkins, 2005:254). As it can be seen from explanations, these technologies are manufacturing technologies. But technology is not only utilized by manufacturing businesses. There are service businesses as well. Therefore, another classification has been made based on the type of organization in that manner. Manufacturing organizations are related with the transformation of inputs into physical outputs, and the technology used in this process is called manufacturing technology. On the other hand, service organizations are the ones that provide nontangible facilities like transportation or consultancy (Madura, 2004:4). Therefore, the way of providing this service can also be regarded as technology. Some organizations are not pure service or manufacturing organizations. In that case, both technologies can be used together. Another classification of technology has been made by Thompson, and this time both manufacturing and service organizations were taken into consideration. This classification has been made based on the interdependence and coordination between units, and technology has been categorized under three types, namely, long-linked, mediating, and intensive technologies (Thompson, 1967:15–17). In *long-linked technology*, organization units are serially interdependent. There is a fixed sequence of steps in the production process. Therefore, the latter step can only be accomplished after the former step. A mass production line can be an example of this type (Aldrich & Herker, 1977:222). In *mediating technology*, different customer groups are linked with each other. For example, commercial banks link depositors and borrowers to each other. Additionally, *intensive technology* is regarded as a custom technology where all units are in reciprocal interdependence with each other. Since the object (here the patient) and units (polyclinics, laboratory, surgery, etc.) are in relation with each other, hospitals can be an example of this type of technology (Thompson, 1967:17). Although there are such basic technology classifications, there are also different subconcepts of technology based on the functional areas of businesses. For example, a design technology (Ohnuma, Tsudaka, Kawahira, & Nozawa, 1998:6686), a production technology (Darr, Argote, & Epple, 1995:1750), or an HR technology (Thornton & Byham, 2013:3,4) can be regarded as functional technologies. Today, with the emergence of the information age, information technology has also taken an important role as supporting a great variety of business activities. Information technology involves information processing and handling support such as computer hardware, software, and communication and information system tools (Lin, Vassar, & Clark, 2011:25), and some organization-wide systems like ERP use information and communication technologies intensively.

Classified under whatever classification, technology is a stubborn part of any business process and is subject to continuous developments. In order to keep up with these developments, organizations try to get new technologies. But the implementation of new technologies may not always result in expected results. Therefore, adoption of technology needs careful decision making.

1.3   Technology adoption process

Technology adoption has been used with different meanings by different researchers in the literature. Some researchers regarded technology adoption as an "organization's receptivity to an innovation and change," while some researchers defined the term as "widespread acceptance, or diffusion, of the innovation throughout an organization or relevant social system" (Neeley, 2006:7). Although the term is mostly defined with the aforementioned explanations, adoption can not only be taken as an acquisition and diffusion of new technology. Since the main issue starts after bringing this new technology into a different organizational setting, it is more appropriate for the term "technology adoption" to be explained with the inclusion of implementation and integration as well.

Process studies that investigate the topic considered technology adoption as a type of decision and explained it with a sequential process. As the new technology adoption process can result in important organizational outcomes, it can be thought as a kind of strategic decision or at least it should be. In one of these process explanations, Mintzberg's decision-making process has been taken and the technology adoption process has been categorized under three steps, namely, identification, development, and selection (Langley & Truax, 1994:622). The *identification process* is related with recognition and diagnosis activities. In this step, the need for a new technology has been realized, and the current status of the organization's technology is investigated. The *development process* is related with search and design activities. In this step, a new technology can be searched based on the requirements detected in the first step. Last, the *selection process* is related with evaluation and approval activities. In this step, a final selection decision is made, and the chosen technology is acquired by the organization. This adoption process ends with the choice of the new technology. However, as stated earlier, integration is also important for the technology adoption process. Therefore, similar to the technology innovation process of Mirvis, Sales, and Hackett (1991), implementation, integration (adoption in the model), and diffusion processes can be included to the new technology adoption process.

The technology adoption process starts with *awareness*. First, the need for a new technology should arise. This may be because of a performance gap between current status and the required one. A performance gap can be realized after a comparison with the competitor, facing unmet objectives or losing market share. As well as realization of a performance gap, acceptance of this gap is also important. Most of the time, it is difficult for managers to accept the fact that their organization fell behind its competitors (Mirvis et al., 1991:116). After this step, *investigating* the current status and determining the requirements follow. This step is similar to the aforementioned *identification* step. Each organization's performance gap can be in different areas. One can have quality problems while the other has communication and coordination problems. Based on the problem, the relevant technology solution also changes. Therefore, it is important to diagnose the organization well before deciding on which technology to adopt (Estrin, Foreman, & Garcia-Miller, 2003:18). After investigation, the requirements are known. Therefore, a suitable technology is *searched* for improvements in specified performance gaps or the organization. In this step, alternative technologies are determined (Mirvis et al., 1991:116,117). This can be made via a benchmarking process with competitors or different industry organizations (Bruque & Moyano, 2007:249). In the search process, criteria are important. Although its functional performance is critical, the cost of this new technology can also be a criterion. In the next step, the decision of new technology is made based on preset criteria and the chosen technology is acquired (Bruque & Moyano, 2007:249). Of course, the *selection and acquisition* of the new technology is not the end of this process. After acquisition, the *implementation and integration* step starts (Farrukh & Probert, 2015:97). Implementation of a new technology can be made as a pilot or organization-wide implementation based on the technology type. As it will also be explained in subsequent sections,

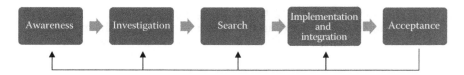

Figure 1.1 Technology adoption process.

readiness toward a new technology is critical for implementation. This is also related with the integration issue. Integration refers to the harmonization of this new technology with the existing organizational setting. When taking the whole technology adoption process into consideration, maybe the most critical one is the integration step, because most of the technology projects end up with failure because organizations underestimate the importance of the integration step. The last step is the *acceptance* step. This is also related with diffusion. If there is a successful integration process, this new technology is accepted and utilized with relevant units in the organization (Ammenwerth, Iller, & Mahler, 2006:2). After utilization of this new technology, necessary improvements are made based on the user feedback (see Figure 1.1).

However, not all the time this process is followed, and some incongruence occurs between the new technology and the current organizational context. Therefore, top management should be careful in technology selection and integration (Knight, 2015).

1.4   *Drivers and barriers of technology adoption*

Adoption of a new technology begins with low rates, and as more and more organizations implement these technologies, this rate accelerates. This tendency of organizations is explained with the technology adoption curve. According to this curve, early adopters of a community make 13.5% of all organizations and over 50% implements this new technology after early adopters (Butler & Sellbom, 2002:22,23). Adoption of a new technology can be affected by many factors. Different from process studies, variance studies search for underlying reasons of technology adoption and its success (Langley & Truax, 1994:620). Drivers or barriers of technology adoption can be classified as internal and external factors. External factors come mostly from the industrial environment of an organization such as pressure of competition. On the other hand, internal factors are called as organizational factors and investigated under several subcategories such as leadership or financial condition.

As stated in the process of technology adoption, first, there should be a reason to adopt new technology. Therefore, leadership is critical.

Top management's characteristics and viewpoints determine this choice and actually all of the processes (Thong & Yap, 1995:429–442). For the realization of the need for technology development, the leader should be monitoring internal and external environments continuously. Therefore, an innovative and open-minded approach is needed. Aside from this, he or she should accept new requirements and allocate a budget for this. These kinds of developments need time and effort. Therefore, patience and commitment are also important as drivers for the technology adoption process (Langley & Truax, 1994:631). Top management should believe in the process and also link new technology adoption with strategy.

As it is also related with investigation, realization of needs for improvement can be regarded among driving forces. In order to do that, employee participation and empowerment can be useful (Mirvis et al., 1991:125). Again top management can maintain these working conditions and encourage feedback.

Organization size can also be both a driver and a barrier to technology adoption. The financial position of small firms affects even their technology search activities. Poor financial position prevents these organizations from adopting new technologies (Fletcher, Wright, & Desai, 1996:12). On the other hand, growing businesses may need to develop their technologies, which can be a driving force for them. Time and competitive pressure can also inhibit the adoption process and result in wrong decisions.

There may be some driving or preventing forces in the implementation and integration process as well. As it will be explained in detail in the next section, the fit between the new technology and organizational context is very important for the success of the technology adoption process. A failure in integration will also affect the acceptance and diffusion of the technology (Ammenwerth et al., 2006:1).

Resistance to change is a strong barrier to technology adoption. In order to prevent this, knowledge is critical. This knowledge can be related with the benefits of this new technology as well as user knowledge. When perceived benefits are communicated well, acceptance will be positively affected (Kitchell, 1995:198). Besides, user-friendly specifications of new technology and training programs for the use of new technologies can be driving forces of new technology adoption (Estrin et al., 2003:25).

As it can be seen from the explanations earlier throughout the technology adoption process, there may be some obstacles in each step. Therefore, it should be evaluated carefully and planned accordingly.

1.5   *Integration of new technologies*

Early studies of the organization theory have researched the relationship between technology and organization in the context of the structural contingency theory (Pfeffer, 1997:158). One of these researches has been conducted by Trist and Bamforth, and it has been seen that organizations are sociotechnical systems (Kocel, 2005:282). In general, a system is defined as a whole comprised of subsystems that interact with each other and also with an upper system (Ulgen & Mirze, 2006:29). Organizations are also systems that interact with their internal and external environment. Sociotechnical systems, on the other hand, are explained with the degree of fit between the work technology and sociopsychological factors existing in the work organization. Organizations are living systems, and high productivity is dependent on how one organization can design its work organization while considering compatibility with the social system (Tompkins, 2005:247). Based on this approach, it can be seen that adoption of a new technology has its effects on organization, and therefore in order to be successful, the necessary alignment should be made for this technology. When integration of a new technology is taken into consideration, it is important to note that there are several factors for effective implementation.

One of these factors is *strategy and technology integration* in the organization. A strategy is "the way, in which an organization endeavors to differentiate itself from its competitors, using its relative corporate strengths to better meet customer needs" (Ohmae, 1982 as cited in Lin et al., 2011:26). Strategy is determined based on the organization's vision and mission, and in the strategy formulation process, both internal and external environment factors are taken into consideration. Since strategic management aims at above-average returns in the long run, it is important to link business processes with strategy in order to achieve better organizational performance (Somers & Nelson, 2003:317). The same is also valid for new technology adoption. Strategy and technology adoption linkage is regarded as a critical success factor in the literature (Fui-Hoon Nah, Lau, & Kuang, 2001:288), because simply applying a new technology does not necessarily bring success to the organization. Even if it may bring success, it may lose its advantages in the long run (Lin et al., 2011:26). Therefore for a better performance, the technology adoption process should be linked to corporate strategy and a clear strategy should be determined (Fletcher & Wright, 1995:116). In this context, organizations can prepare their technology adoption plans along with their corporate strategy. Estrin et al. (2003) explained the preparation of the technology adoption plan with a seven-step process. It starts with articulation of a corporate strategy. In this step, the strategy provides a direction for the organization. In the second step, a linkage between strategy and technology is formed. Here, the technology strategy that supports the corporate strategy is determined. For example, if an organization is growing in different geographical areas, the coordination and communication needs between different units may require a comprehensive technology adoption strategy. Based on these steps, in subsequent steps the current status is analyzed, a vision is developed, a road map for this vision is prepared, technology alternatives are evaluated, and technology and business process changes are implemented (Estrin et al., 2003:14). A strategic focus to technology adoption increases commitment and makes top management support possible. Integration with the strategy can also show the contribution of this new technology to corporate strategy, and therefore, it can be improved to support organizational performance.

Another important issue in technology adoption is *integration of technology with structure*. A formal organizational structure can be defined as a set of deliberate arrangements of organizational setting. Organizational design, task and job specifications, hierarchical levels, reporting, and command patterns are all examples of organizational structure factors (Yurur, 2015:14–17). Organizational design is related with the way of grouping tasks and jobs. Functional organizations or team organizations are examples of this. Each design bears different structural specifications in itself. While functional organizations are based on specialization and formalization, team-based organizations are based on coordination and collaboration. Hierarchical levels (flat or steep), decision authority (centralized or decentralized), or the level of complexity is also part of the design issue (Fletcher et al., 1996:13). Organizational design has taken the attention of researchers, and many of them have searched the relationship between technology and structure. Results of these researches show that the utilized technology shapes the structure of an organization (Kocel, 2005:282). Adopting a new technology brings a need for change (Fletcher & Wright, 1995:125) and requires redesign of tasks as well (Somers & Nelson, 2003:319). A new technology may change the way and sequence of working or it may even change the layout of the work environment. These changes can be related with the physical settings, responsibilities, or work politics. Therefore in the integration process, alignment of the structure also has a critical importance (Fui-Hoon Nah et al., 2001:288). If there is a need for change in the physical work setting, organizations can utilize business process reengineering (BPR) (Ngai, Law, & Wat, 2008:551). In this way, they can arrange the work flow from scratch accordingly. But this process is not always easy. Since organizations are sociotechnical systems, the needs of employees cannot be ignored as well. They do not want to lose their control over their jobs or may not want to be socially isolated (if needed). Fear of job or power loss creates resistance to change (Somers & Nelson, 2003:123). Lack of knowledge about new technology can also be a barrier to successful adoption of technology. For a successful redesign, organizations should inform their employees and give the necessary training required by the new technology (Knight, 2015). Forming a special team or function for the management of this technology can also be useful (Bruque & Moyano, 2007:244). Without the necessary adjustments, failure of an organization is inevitable with an incompatible technology and structure.

With regard to the technology–structure integration, another critical issue in the adoption of new technologies is *technology and culture integration*. Managing change that comes with the adoption of a new technology is closely related with the culture of an organization. Organizational culture is defined as "a set of key values, beliefs, understandings that are shared by members of an organization" (Smircich, 1983 as cited in Lin et al., 2011:27). In the technology adoption process, readiness of the organization plays an important role and necessary culture constitutes a part of this (Fink, 1998:246). First, in the adoption of a technology, one of the most important cultural issues can be thought as the approach of top management (Lin et al., 2011:27), because supportiveness of top management facilitates the acceptance process of new technology. Any change in the organization may lead to confusion and anxiety; therefore, management should be able to handle this situation well. As stated earlier, there may be lack of knowledge for the new technology, but if an organization has a learning-oriented culture, it will not be reluctant to invest in HR development (Blotnicky, 2009:47), and as a result adaptation will be easy. As well as learning orientation, trust is also important (Mirvis et al., 1991:116,117). The reason for the change with its consequences should be communicated with employees. In order to make necessary justifications, the feedback of users plays a critical role in the integration process. With this, a culture with participation and open communication should be maintained by the organization (Bruque & Moyano, 2007:242).

Integration of a new technology has a critical role for organizations and one factor cannot be thought as separate from another. All these issues are embedded and related with one another. For this reason, for a successful adoption process, organizations should be aware of this reality.

1.6   Conclusion

As a result of fierce competition, businesses are searching for new technologies to better serve their customers in the industry. Technological developments are taking place in many areas of businesses and providing advantages for both organizations and consumers. With the help of implemented technologies, organizations can integrate and automate their business processes (Fui-Hoon Nah et al., 2001:285), increase the necessary information flow and coordination between different units (Lin et al., 2011:25), make operation control (i.e., stock control) more efficient and accurate (Fletcher & Wright, 1995:115), and better manage their business processes. As a result of these advantages, organizations can increase their efficiency, effectiveness, and performance (Fink, 1998:244). However, in order to benefit from these advantages, organization–technology fit plays the most important factor (Estrin et al., 2003:4). Therefore in this context, for creating this fit, new technology should be integrated with the strategy, structure, and culture of the organization.

Today, many organizations are implementing a new technology just because competitors did so, or because it is popular. But it is important to note that without the necessary alignment of new technology with these organizational factors, it cannot go beyond an expense for organizations. Besides, a proactive and strategic approach can provide an insight for understanding the interrelations between different critical organizational factors.

The technology adoption process is comprised of several phases such as awareness, investigation, search, implementation and integration, and acceptance. Each step is important for the success of adoption, but one of these phases is much more critical. That is the integration step. In this context, as stated earlier, forming the link between strategy and technology is important, because with this strategy–technology link, the adoption process will be held more systematically and controlled properly. Besides, as well as the importance the process will gain, it will be possible to assess its contribution to corporate vision as well. Integration of new technology with the structure is also another issue that should be taken into consideration. Structure is mostly explained with authority and power. This new technology may require a change in the way of doing the work, responsibilities, or formal communication patterns. Therefore in such a situation, necessary adoptions should be made by organizations. A new technology adoption, minimal or radical, brings some changes together, and in a change situation there is always a risk of resistance. In this vein, organizational culture plays an important role. In a culture with openness to advancements, open communication, collaboration, and trust, it will be easier to accept and implement this new technology. Therefore, a technology that is incontinent with the culture bears a high risk of failure.

Whether a new technology brings change in the structure or social setting, it should not be forgotten that organizations are sociotechnical systems. Therefore, balance between the technical and social setting should not be ignored, and managers should be aware that for the success of this process, alignment is a fatal necessity. In this context, this chapter provides an insight for this critical issue; also, based on the theoretical basis provided here, it creates a research avenue on the topic of technology adoption. Although there are various variance and process studies in the literature, this study brings a different perspective and explains the role of organizational factors on this process based on each step (see Section 1.4). However, as a further study, empirical researches that investigate this role based on each step would also be useful.

References

Aldrich, H., & Herker, D. (1977). Boundary spanning roles and organization structure. *Academy of Management Review, 2*(2), 217–230.

Ammenwerth, E., Iller, C., & Mahler, C. (2006). IT-adoption and the interaction of task, technology and individuals: A fit framework and a case study. *BMC Medical Informatics and Decision Making, 6*(1), 1–13.

Blau, P. M., Falbe, C. M., McKinley, W., & Tracy, P. K. (1976). Technology and organization in manufacturing. *Administrative Science Quarterly, 21*, 20–40.

Blotnicky, K. A. (2009). *Examining the impact of marketing orientation on information technology adoption in Canadian firms.* Northcentral University, Prescott Valley, AZ.

Bruque, S., & Moyano, J. (2007). Organisational determinants of information technology adoption and implementation in SMEs: The case of family and cooperative firms. *Technovation, 27*(5), 241–253.

Butler, D. L., & Sellbom, M. (2002). Barriers to adopting technology. *Educause Quarterly, 2*, 22–28.

Darr, E. D., Argote, L., & Epple, D. (1995). The acquisition, transfer, and depreciation of knowledge in service organizations: Productivity in franchises. *Management Science, 41*(11), 1750–1762.

Estrin, L., Foreman, J. T., & Garcia-Miller, S. (2003). Overcoming barriers to technology adoption in small manufacturing enterprises (SMEs). Technical Report, Carnegie Mellon Software Engineering Institute, Pitssburg PA, Technology Insertion Demonstration and Evaluation Program repository.cmu.edu/cgi/viewcontent.cgi?article=1219&context=sei

Farrukh, C., & Probert, D. (2015). Managing technology and knowledge across organisational interfaces. In L. Morel-Guimaraes, Y. A. Hosni, & T. M. Khalil (Eds.), *Management of technology: Key success factors for innovation and sustainable development: Selected papers from the twelfth International Conference on Management of Technology,* pp. 97–108. Amsterdam, The Netherlands: Elsevier.

Fink, D. (1998). Guidelines for the successful adoption of information technology in small and medium enterprises. *International Journal of Information Management, 18*(4), 243–253.

Fletcher, K., & Wright, G. (1995). Organizational, strategic and technical barriers to successful implementation of database marketing. *International Journal of Information Management, 15*(2), 115–126.

Fletcher, K., Wright, G., & Desai, C. (1996). The role of organizational factors in the adoption and sophistication of database marketing in the UK financial services industry. *Journal of Direct Marketing, 10*(1), 10–21.

Fui-Hoon Nah, F., Lee-Shang Lau, J., & Kuang, J. (2001). Critical factors for successful implementation of enterprise systems. *Business Process Management Journal, 7*(3), 285–296.

Hickson, D. J., Pugh, D. S., & Pheysey, D. C. (1969). Operations technology and organization structure: An empirical reappraisal. *Administrative Science Quarterly, 14*, 378–397.

Kitchell, S. (1995). Corporate culture, environmental adaptation, and innovation adoption: A qualitative/quantitative approach. *Journal of the Academy of Marketing Science, 23*(3), 195–205.

Knight, R. (2015). Convincing skeptical employees to adopt new technology. *Harvard Business Review,* March 19, 2015, Retrieved on March 20, 2015. https://hbr.org/2015/03/convincing-skeptical-employees-to-adopt-new-technology.

Kocel, T. (2005). "Isletme Yoneticiligi", Arikan Basimevi, Istanbul, Turkiye.

Langley, A., & Truax, J. (1994). A process study of new technology adoption in smaller manufacturing firms. *Journal of Management Studies, 31*(5), 619–652.

Lin, B., Vassar, J. A., & Clark, L. S. (2011). Information technology strategies for small businesses. *Journal of Applied Business Research (JABR), 9*(2), 25–29.

Madura, J. (2004). *Introduction to business.* Canada: Thompson/South-Western.

Mirvis, P. H., Sales, A. L., & Hackett, E. J. (1991). The implementation and adoption of new technology in organizations: The impact on work, people, and culture. *Human Resource Management, 30*(1), 113–139.

Neeley, C. K. R. (2006). Connective technology adoption in the supply chain: The role of organizational, interorganizational and technology-related factors. Doctoral Dissertation, University of North Texas, TX.

Ngai, E. W., Law, C. C., & Wat, F. K. (2008). Examining the critical success factors in the adoption of enterprise resource planning. *Computers in Industry, 59*(6), 548–564.

Ohmae, K. (1982). *The mind of the strategist.* New York: McGraw-Hill.

Ohnuma, H., Tsudaka, K., Kawahira, H., & Nozawa, S. (1998). Lithography computer aided design technology for embedded memory in logic. *Japanese Journal of Applied Physics, 37*(12S), 6686–6688.

Pfeffer, J. (1997). *New directions for organization theory: Problems and prospects.* New York: Oxford University Press.

Somers, T. M., & Nelson, K. G. (2003). The impact of strategy and integration mechanisms on enterprise system value: Empirical evidence from manufacturing firms. *European Journal of Operational Research, 146*(2), 315–338.

Thompson, J. D. (1967). *Organizations in action: Social science bases of administrative theory.* New York: McGraw-Hill.

Thong, J. Y., & Yap, C. S. (1995). CEO characteristics, organizational characteristics and information technology adoption in small businesses. *Omega, 23*(4), 429–442.

Thornton III, G. C., & Byham, W. C. (1982). *Assessment centers and managerial performance.* New York: Academic Press, Inc.

Tompkins, J. (2005). *Organization theory and public management.* Belmont, CA: Thomson/Wadsworth Publishing Company.

Ulgen, H., & Mirze, S. K. (2006). Isletmelerde Stratejik Yonetim, Literatür Yayınevi, 3rd Edition, Istanbul/TURKIYE.

Yurur, S., Orgut Kurami ve Tasarimina Giris. (2015). Cev. Ed. Timurcanday Ozmen, O.N., Orgut Kuramlari ve Tasarimini Anlamak (Nobel Yayinevi), pp. 2–51, Ankara, Turkiye.

chapter two

Technological and organizational changes
Challenges for HRM

José Manuel Gameiro Rebelo dos Santos
and Maria Amélia Marques

Contents

Abstract

This chapter refers to some of the implications for human resource management that result from changes occurring due to globalization and the adoption of new technologies in the organizational world.

From a macro-perspective, it is possible to identify two opposing trends: a reduction of jobs due to increased automation and the use of sophisticated technology and another one resulting in manpower shortage due to an aging population, leading to a situation in which the number of individuals available to join the labor market will be much lower than the number of individuals retiring. While the reduction of jobs contributes to the increase in the unemployment rate, population aging allows to foresee a substantial decrease in unemployment in the coming years, even if the number of jobs diminishes.

At the micro-level, three conceptualizations of human resource management indissociable from the changes taking place are identified: as representing a new conceptualization of the personnel function; as an evolution and an embellishment of personnel administration; and as mere rhetoric or mere language difference that aims to convey a set of "White, Anglo-Saxon, Protestant" (WASP) values, such as individualism and work ethics, and to credit the personnel function. Human resource practices associated with these conceptualizations cannot be dissociated from the current conjecture.

Keywords: New technologies, labor market, human resource management, human resource practices

2.1   Introduction

Globalization, the increase of economic competition, and the differentiation of consumption mutually conditioned by technological and employment innovations, as well as the change in work settings, have presented organizations with new challenges in what concerns the management of people. In highly competitive environments, organizations are challenged with the need to be more proactive, that is, to be able to anticipate and/or to respond with efficacy and efficiency to rapid technological and market changes. These changes imply that companies ought to simplify their organizational structures, promote the autonomy of employees to ensure functional flexibility, enhance learning and creativity, and, in accordance with the latter, shift the managing of people through norms and rules to management through culture and/or commitment (Crozier, 1994; Walton, 1985).

Since the 1980s, companies have been facing a number of challenges that have focused on the need to conceptualize the managing of people at work in new ways.

People considered as human resources and/or as strategic assets of the organization require new work settings to develop their skills and more advanced human resource management (HRM) practices that promote their training and development. However, although the need to adopt new forms of work practices and new HRM models appears to be consensual and disseminated in the academic and entrepreneurial discourse, the adoption of the prescribed practices in some national and sectorial contexts is far from what is expected.

Thus, we emphasize the importance of contextual factors in shaping organizational practices in general and HRM practices in particular. In Europe, the "fit" between organizational strategy and HRM strategy is generally ambiguous or unclear (Gooderham et al., 2004).

In general, the adoption of new alternative work practices stems more from the need to comply with legal requirements, that is, institutional isomorphism (Dimaggio and Powell, 1983), than from the definition of a competitive organizational strategy sustained on strategic human resource management (SHRM). In Portugal, despite the increasing adoption of more advanced HRM and alternative work practices, there is still a perseverance of traditional personnel management as well as more traditional work organization models. Notwithstanding what was said, there are significant differences related to several factors, such as the sector of activity and the type and size of the firm.

Currently, Europe is facing a number of social and economic challenges. The economic crisis is accompanied by the unprecedented technological boom. Portugal in particular has been living the last few years under a climate of austerity and of rapid social and economic changes, being the most obvious the soaring of emigration of highly qualified workers, the increase of unemployment, and the elimination of a considerable number of job posts, the latter due to the bankruptcy and/or close of a considerable number of companies and also due to the restructuring of work itself. Notwithstanding this and despite the tendency for the persistence of more traditional forms of work organization and HRM practices, there appears to be an increase in the adoption of more advanced work practices.

Having said this, the main aim of this chapter is to bring about certain topics of reflection concerning some of the factors that shape HRM models.

2.2   Internationalization, globalization, and its consequences

Internationalization of companies and globalization brought about new challenges for people, companies, and society. Globalization can be understood as a phenomenon that is economic and also political, technological, and cultural (Giddens, 2000). There are thus visible impacts in the society that lead to its reconfiguration.

Globalization can be translated in highly complex movements that are characterized, among other aspects, by the opening of borders as well as deregulation (Giddens, 2000). Globalization refers to the spread of practical and theoretical knowledge as well as products from any place in the world, affecting transversally every individual and society and having social, political, and economic implications (Gouveia et al., 2009).

Especially from the 1970s onward, globalization is at play in the evolution of information systems (Giddens, 2000).

This way, organizations can redefine the ways in which they produce and commercialize their goods and services, assuming that there are advantageous results emerging out of that redefinition. As a result, we observe increased economic interdependence and increased competitiveness. This produces concerns in what regards organization of work and how to source cheap labor for less qualified work posts. These changes are all due to market globalization, technological evolution, and demographical changes—in particular, population aging (Bruggeman et al., 2012).

Technologies have been implying a redefinition of the ideas of time and space that is translated in substantial changes within the organizations (Costa, 2012). Thus, technological development has been contributing to the dismissal of borders between multiple sectors of activity. As a result, sectors that would appear to have nothing in common often end up relating to each other (António, 2015).

This leads to a broader perspective of the sectors of activity. In today's context they can be conceptualized as "societal sectors" (Scott and Meyer, 1983) that are functional and not geographical, that is, they are represented not only by the set of organizations that operate in the same field and that can be identified by the similarity of their services, products, and functions but also by the organizations that influence significantly their performance and/or activity such as suppliers, clients, and competitors (Scott and Meyer, 1983).

Enabled by technology advancement and the subsequent creation of information systems and networks, globally, companies have been adopting the "flexible firm" model (Atkinson, 1984) by focusing on their core business and outsourcing all other activities. Thus, the workforce has been divided into two groups: core workers (employees that are key for the business because they are perceived as having high value and singularity and thus need to be retained, trained, and developed) and peripheral workers (employees perceived of low value and singularity and not core for the business and thus do not need to be retained or developed).

When companies internationalize, they usually keep their core workers and core activities, for example, those involving R&D, in their mother country and move their less demanding cognitive skill activities to countries where labor is cheaper and/or considered more peripheral.

Some experts claim that in the future the Western world will focus on the development of sophisticated products while less developed countries will produce elementary goods (Michelin et al., 2003), which will or may lead to the enhancement of this division between countries as to their development of innovation as well as labor.

Notwithstanding this, the internationalization to some developing countries has also led to the need of expatriation and to subsequent repatriation. Expatriation can be defined as temporary dislocation of mostly highly qualified individuals to another country to exercise a professional activity for a company they are integrated in (Edwards and Rees, 2006; Rego and Cunha, 2009). Frequently, expatriation happens with the change of location of the company itself or with one of its production unities. To ensure the control of such a company or unity there is the need to send someone with the technical skills and the ability to adapt to a different culture. Repatriation is the reverse movement, the coming back of individuals to the original country and company, after having worked abroad as expatriates.

These trends bring about new challenges for HRM that can briefly be described as the need to manage multicultural groups (Bertrán, 2015) and, as we will discuss ahead, to identify and understand the contextual factors, beyond the cultural factors, that shape HRM models.

As a result of the globalization and dislocation, we can observe that in the Western world labor costs are diminishing, even when labor is highly qualified, and there is an increase of unemployment, aggravated by the economic crisis. Youth are a particularly vulnerable group.

When looking for short- to medium-term solutions to minimize unemployment, the answer lies in small and medium companies (SME) as the ones that can contribute more to new types of jobs throughout the Western world (Melo and Machado, 2015). However, these appear to the ones that have more difficulty in introducing more advanced HRM models (Claus, 2003), due to the lack of an HR department and/or specific competences in this field, as well as to formalize practices (Claus, 2003; Veloso and Keating, 2008), assuring the transparency of procedures and equal rights.

This context appears to be very noticeable in Portugal, with the increased sense of insecurity and less attractive job conditions, in particular in what concerns compensations and opportunities for professional development. This happens due to the "deficient work and labor market conditions, the low productivity of our [Portuguese] companies and the lack of qualifications and education from decision-making politicians, workers, CEOs and managers alike" (Centeno, 2013: 17).

This scenario can be looked at from a macro-perspective to talk about labor markets and the evolution of employment or unemployment. On the other hand, we can look at it from a micro-perspective to identify and look for the implications of human resource practices that are operating in a set of companies, especially concerning recruiting and selecting, types of contracts and contractual conditions, and remunerations.

The labor market and the organizations suffer from different pressures coming from both the technological changes and the lack of incomes (Alis et al., 2014). There appears to be some tension between the extinction of job posts and the need for labor.

Technological changes, automatization, and robotics require less but more qualified labor (Alis et al., 2014), which contribute to the extinction of a considerable number of job posts. For example, this also appears to be one of the reasons that in Portugal even the unemployment rate was less than 4%; in 2001, it rose reaching values higher than 16% (Centeno, 2013). And lately, there are very mild signs that show that unemployment is regressing.

However, this is not to show the merit of an improving economy but rather to illustrate the aforementioned decision of a lot of qualified youth to emigrate to different countries, mainly around Europe. On the other hand, demographical issues allow us to estimate the lack of labor at a medium but also short term—especially in some specific areas.

The implications of technological evolution in the productive capacity that organizations have are not new. The speed at which that occurs is the factor that has increased greatly, generating equipment obsolescence and making planning difficult.

The consequences of incorporation of machinery and more automated mechanisms have always been a source of concern since it implies less labor to produce the same amount of goods.

Particularly, smaller companies that relied on intense and badly paid labor where human work could be easily replaced by machines gained plenty of profit for undergoing this change. A company cannot be kept artificially merely to preserve work posts because there are obvious competitive losses making the situation unsustainable. In cases in which this is the option chosen the very survival of the company can be at stake.

As a result, we have some job posts that are eliminated through this mean. Yet, the decrease in nonqualified labor needs, characterized by nongratifying and repetitive activities, has been counterbalanced by the increase in needs for qualified labor to conceive and manage the new equipment. The readjustment of HRM practices that has been happening in bigger companies is in great deal a result of automation.

A part of these readjustments is about workers adapting to technological change, operationalization of strategic planning, networking, and total quality, being that these now become elements of their new reality. As a result, new instruments that facilitate HRM were developed (Alis et al., 2014), and monitoring is then changed to frameworks that are adapted to the organizations' new reality.

Small to medium companies often cannot access the instruments to face the new reality. Even though they are still the organizations that generate more jobs (Alis et al., 2014), they lack critical mass, capacity for effective planning, and defining strategies of work sustainability.

In plenty of cases, not even an automated structure to manage human resources is available. Even though little information is available regarding HRM in SME in Portugal, some recent studies note that ⅔ do not do human resource planning—though most of them develop some practices in what comes to recruitment and selection (Melo and Machado, 2015).

The training is also an aspect that changes here. Certain elements start being part of the daily life of small to medium companies—the diagnosis of needs and the elaboration and operationalization of the training plan. The evaluation of the training itself has lower priority (Melo and Machado, 2015).

These organizations apparently are conscious of the importance of HRM. However, their practices are not very developed and lack articulation and alignment with the organizational strategy. Frequently, they rely on informal mechanisms that do not stand up to the high levels of development (Melo and Machado, 2015).

2.3 Demographic pressure

From a macro-perspective, the labor market is under two distinct pressures: a technological one (previously approached), which points to a reduction of job posts, and a demographic one, which points the other way: the increase in population aging and the decreased number of births makes the workers hard to replace.

The tendency has been to increase retirement age for the sake of sustainability. This is tightly connected to the increase in life expectancy, the diminishing active population, and the lack of labor that replaces the ones who leave the job market. In addition, youth available to take up free spaces in the job market and replace those who are retiring are insufficient in number.

This tendency is predicted to worsen over the next years being that they are a reflection of the births of the last 5 years of the twentieth century.

In Portugal, the projections by the National Statistics Institute between the period between 2012 and 2060 predicting a high, a central, and a low scenario (Instituto Nacional de Estatística, 2014) show that (1) the high scenario assumes an optimistic evolution for fertility, mortality, and migrations (this means moderate increase in birth, increase in life expectancy, and positive net migration with higher immigrants than emigrants); (2) the central scenario assumes that birth rate increases more modestly, life expectancy increases slightly, and net migration is again positive; and (3) the low scenario assumes that fertility rate is similar to the current ones (1.3 per woman), mortality is in line with present values, and net migrations are also similar to the negative net migration rates that are currently seen.

For practical reasons, we are only considering the period between 2012 and 2027. To analyze the demographic pressure, let us suppose that individuals go into the job market at the age of 20 and retire at the age of 66. Let us also suppose that the economic activities stand at a similar level, not creating nor destructing positions. From the previous data, no matter the type of scenario (Tables 2.1 through 2.3), the number of individuals who retire at the age of 66 is always substantially higher than the number of individuals entering the job market.

The only difference is the deficit created during this period (between 2012 and 2027), which varies between 330,000 (Table 2.4) and 357,000 (Table 2.3) (Instituto Nacional de Estatística, 2014).

There is evidence that the number of people leaving is higher than the number of people who want to enter the labor market even assuming that some job posts will be eliminated due to technological evolution.

Assumedly there will be a high decrease in the current unemployment rates and an increase in difficulty in finding labor. This can lead to individuals to stay in the job market longer and an increase in work costs.

Table 2.1 Scenario 1

Scenario 1 low	20 years old	66 years old	Differential	Accumulated
2012	114,044	113,852	−192	−192
2013	111,967	113,377	1,410	1,218
2014	106,582	125,673	19,091	20,309
2015	106,078	122,528	16,450	36,759
2016	106,379	124,946	18,567	55,326
2017	106,924	126,712	19,788	75,114
2017	107,081	126,705	19,624	94,738
2019	110,163	123,889	13,726	108,464
2020	112,542	126,580	14,038	122,502
2021	103,143	130,253	27,110	149,612
2022	103,610	128,742	25,132	174,744
2023	102,722	132,322	29,600	204,344
2024	100,006	133,613	33,607	237,951
2025	101,530	133,625	32,095	270,046
2026	97,619	139,542	41,923	311,969
2027	95,019	140,262	45,243	357,212

Source: Adapted from Instituto Nacional de Estatística (INE), Projeções de população residente 2012–2060, www.ine.pt (consultado a February 25, 2015), 2014.

Table 2.2 Scenario 2

Scenario 2 medium	20 years old	66 years old	Differential	Accumulated
2012	114,044	113,852	−192	−192
2013	112,195	113,413	1,218	1,026
2014	107,139	125,767	18,628	19,654
2015	107,008	122,698	15,690	35,344
2016	107,693	125,206	17,513	52,857
2017	108,615	127,075	18,460	71,317
2017	109,132	127,182	18,050	89,367
2019	112,562	124,491	11,929	101,296
2020	115,272	127,316	12,044	113,340
2021	106,196	131,129	24,933	138,273
2022	106,979	129,767	22,788	161,061
2023	106,402	133,505	27,103	188,164
2024	103,993	134,960	30,967	219,131
2025	105,823	135,146	29,323	248,454
2026	102,219	141,245	39,026	287,480
2027	99,925	142,154	42,229	329,709

Source: Adapted from Instituto Nacional de Estatística (INE), Projeções de população residente 2012–2060, www.ine.pt (consultado a February 25, 2015), 2014.

Table 2.3 Scenario 3

Scenario 3 high	20 years old	66 years old	Differential	Accumulated
2012	114,044	113,852	−192	−192
2013	112,198	113,450	1,252	1,060
2014	107,145	125,885	18,740	19,800
2015	107,020	122,895	15,875	35,675
2016	107,709	125,502	17,793	53,468
2017	108,636	127,473	18,837	72,305
2017	109,157	127,680	18,523	90,828
2019	112,591	125,075	12,484	103,312
2020	115,307	128,012	12,705	116,017
2021	106,232	131,945	25,713	141,730
2022	107,018	130,669	23,651	165,381
2023	106,443	134,526	28,083	193,464
2024	104,035	136,084	32,049	225,513
2025	105,869	136,361	30,492	256,005
2026	102,266	142,606	40,340	296,345
2027	99,972	143,609	43,637	339,982

Source: Adapted from Instituto Nacional de Estatística (INE), Projeções de população residente 2012–2060, www.ine.pt (consultado a February 25, 2015), 2014.

Table 2.4 Different perspectives of HRM

Different perspectives	Focus	Authors
Best fit	Causal relationship between HRM and organizational performance	Schuler and Jackson (1987), Miles and Snow (1984), Delery and Doty (1996), Guest (1997), Pfeffer (1994), MacDuffies (1995)
Contextualist	Study the viability of the emergence of a European HRM model. Focus on contextual factors	Brewster (1995), Sparrow and Hilthrop (1997), Claus (2003)
New institutionalism	Factors that influence the similarities and differences between firms	DiMaggio and Powell (1983), Scott and Meyer (1983)
Political	The role of the actors	Pichault and Schoenaers (2003)
Resource based	Focus mainly on internal factors. New approach to strategic HRM	Boxall and Purcell (2000), Kamoche (1996), Lado and Wilson (1994), Lepak and Snell (1999), Grant (1998)

Source: Marques, M.A., *Modelos Organizacionais e Práticas de Gestão de Recursos Humanos: um estudo multi-caso*, Lisboa, Portugal, ISEG-UTL, 2010.

2.4   HRM perspectives

Having looked at organizational changes and challenges at a more macro-level, in this chapter we will focus specifically on HRM models and practices.

Since the 1980s, HRM has been highly recognized by academics and entrepreneurs as a pivotal means to attain competitive advantage. Nevertheless and regardless of the vast research and interventions in this field, HRM has failed to establish itself as a consistent body of knowledge, for it appears to be embedded in some ambiguities and paradoxes. As Keenoy (1997: 825) points out "(…) the more we study HRism, the more we find out about it and the more we elaborate it, the more elusive and obscure it becomes." The lack of consensus is apparent in the discussion about the concept of "HRM" itself.

This discussion can be typified in three conceptualizations or positions regarding the use of the concept "HRM," namely (Marques, 2010): as representing a new conceptualization of the personnel function; as an evolution and an embellishment of personnel administration; as mere rhetoric or mere language difference that aims to convey a set of "White, Anglo-Saxon, Protestant" (WASP) values, such as individualism and work ethics, and to credit the personnel function. As to the first conceptualization of HRM, Storey (1995: 9) considers that what delimits "HRM" from "personnel management" is "(…) that it eschews the joint regulative approach—and even more so the craft regulative approach." Brewster and Larsen (2000: 2) reinforce Storey's (1995) approach, underlining that "(…) the HRM concept attempts to integrate the interplay between individual, task and organization."

Brewster and Larsen (2000) state that the concept has been highly promoted because it is perceived as positive and desirable for organizations and also that it has been given more importance than it actually has in enabling the gain of competitive advantage because it has focused essentially on good practices and results.

As to the second conceptualization of HRM, an evolution and an embellishment of personnel administration, Torrington (1995) considers that "HRM" emerged as a form of "embellishing" and institutionalizing the personnel function and to increase the authority of people that perform this function, making it more "unitary." Consequently, he considers that "HRM" is more centered on strategy and the planning of labor than on the solving of daily problems.

This is done through structured programs, such as corporate culture and team building. Placing themselves in this approach, Mahoney and Dekop (1986) defined some "marks" in the evolution from personnel administration to "HRM," namely, (1) the development of personnel planning, the shift from short-term planning based on present needs to a more strategic and provisionary planning of labor; (2) the shift from indirect to direct participation of workers; (3) the adoption of teamwork as opposed to individual work; (4) the shift from a problem-solving approach to an accountability approach (this enabled the shift from a more individual control [e.g., absenteeism, turnover, job satisfaction] to a broader approach that includes organizational performance and effectiveness); (5) the evolution of the concept of job training, from on-the-job training to the development of competencies and career management; and (6) the shift from the concept of "morale" to that of organizational climate and culture (individual to group).

As to the third conceptualization of HRM, Karen Legge (1995) has a more extremist position. She considers that the difference between "HRM" and personnel administration/management is a mere language difference, the main difference being the aim for the former to convey a set of "WASP" (White, Anglo-Saxon, Protestant) values, such as individualism and work ethics. Legge (1995) also considers that "HRM" focuses more on the way to obtain competitive advantages and is used to credit the personnel function. She points out some differences between HRM and personnel administration, that is, personnel administration is perceived as the exercise of authority by managers over subordinates, thus excluding managers from this type of management, whereas "HRM" presumes that the focus is directed to and by a "team of managers." Another difference is that personnel administration presumes that policies and practices are implemented by the personnel function, whereas "HRM" presumes that they are shared by line management. Last, HRM is based on the principles of corporate culture.

The different conceptualizations of HRM also seem evident in the different perspectives of HRM.

In the different perspectives, there appears to be a shift from a more micro-approach and universalistic approach to HRM to a more macro-approach and holistic approach (Table 2.4).

The shift to a more holistic approach seems to be apparent in the different theories on SHRM. We have named them as the "best-fit" perspectives because they are based on the underlying assumption that there is a causal relationship between HRM practices or systems and organizational performance. The concept of "best fit" is, in this context, polysemous. The "best-fit" can be understood as follows (Wood, 1999): "strategic fit," that is, the fit between HRM practices and organizational or business strategy; "organizational fit," that is, the fit between a set of practices or HRM systems and other systems in the organization; "environmental fit," that is, the fit between HRM practices and external factors; and "internal fit," that is, the coherence of the HRM practice system.

SHRM theories can be typified in three perspectives (Delery and Doty, 1996): universalistic, contingency, and configurational. The universalistic perspective focuses on the identification and recommendation of best practices that will warrant the organization high performance. The other two perspectives focus on defining more holistic models that contain a larger number of variables that shape HRM. The contingency perspectives assume that the relationship between HRM practices and organizational development is shaped by contingency factors, such as organizational size, seniority, technology, capital intensity, sector of activity, the unionization rate, and shareholder.

The contingency perspectives assume that there is a net of complex relationships between HRM variables, HRM variables and contingency factors, and HRM variables and performance indicators, as well as between performance indicators and contingency factors. The configurational perspectives assume that the organizational performance depends on how close the set of HRM practices is to an ideal model of HRM.

Pfeffer's (1994) best practice model is probably the one that best represents the universalistic perspective. The author initially identified 16 best practices and later in 1998 seven practices of success (job security; selective hiring; autonomous work groups; performance linked rewards (high rewards); extensive training; flat organizations (low hierarchical differentiation); sharing of information about organizational performances at all levels), that no matter the context would assure competitive advantages.

Miles and Snow's (1984) model is an example of the contingency approach. The authors "fit" the HRM model with the strategy of each organization (Table 2.5).

Table 2.5 Best-fit perspectives

Best-fit perspectives	Characteristics	Authors
Universalistic	There are a set of practices that assure best performance: "best practices," "high-performance work practices," and "flexible work practices."	Huselid (1995), Pfeffer (1994), Osterman (1994), Guest (1997)
Contingency	The relationship between HRM practices and organizational development is shaped by contingency factors (organizational size, seniority, technology, capital intensity, sector of activity).	Miles and Snow (1984), Schuler and Jackson (1987), Fombrun et al. (1987), Legnick-Hall (1988), Mintzberg (1995)
Configurational	Performance depends on how close the HRM practices are to an ideal model of HRM.	Arthur (1994), MacDuffies (1995)

Source: Adapted from Delery, J.E. and Doty, H.D., *Acad. Manage. J.*, 39(4), 802, 1996.

In their typology, Miles and Snow (1984) identified three types of companies (defenders, analyzers, and prospectors):

- The defenders are organizations that focus on its current markets, maintaining stable growth and serving its current customers and have traditional models of HRM based on collective polices, extensive training, and rewards by professional category.
- The analyzers are organizations that maintain their market share and pursue to be innovative, although usually not as innovative as organizations that have a prospector strategy. These organizations have mixed HRM practices that focus on both the acquisition and development of human resources.
- The prospectors are organizations that are innovative and growth oriented. These organizations explore new markets and new growth opportunities and encourage risk taking. Their HRM models are more individualized and they focus on both the acquisition and development of human resources.

MacDuffies (1995) presents what can be considered a configurational model. Having studied 70 plants in the automobile industry, the author identified what he named as "work innovative practices" that enhance organizational performance. However, according to MacDuffies (1995), the work innovative practices only enhance economic performance if three conditions are met: (1) when workers have skills and knowledge that managers' lack, (2) when workers are willing to mobilize their competences and skills in a discretionary effort, and (3) when the strategy and the performance of the organization are dependent on that discretionary effort.

One of the key points of MacDuffies (1995) model is that he argues that it is the combination of practices or "bundles" that assures the improvement of performance and not the use of isolated practices.

The focus on the combination of set of practices as opposed to the use of isolated practices is one of the unifying points between MacDuffies' (1995), Huselid's (1995) ("high-performance work practices") and Arthur's (1994) ("new working practices") models (Beardwell and Claydon, 2010).

Apart from the difficulty in measuring the effects of "best practices" on organizational performance, because some of the effects of these practices are intangible (Pfeffer, 1997), the effect of the combination or complementarity of practices is another unsolved issue in the "best-fit" perspective. For example, Osterman (1994) and Delaney and Huselid (1996), contrary to MacDuffies (1995), did not find significant differences between the use of complimentary and noncomplimentary HR practices. Moreover, Osterman (1994: 186) also mentions that "At a minimum it seems to me that these data indicate that it is too early to construct' ideal types' of internal labor markets or 'transformed firms."

A more holistic approach on HRM is given by the contextualist perspectives.

The main aims of the contextualist perspectives are to identify and understand the contextual factors that shape HRM practices and to understand the factors that shape the differences between a potential HRM European model and what one could consider the U.S. HRM model (Brewster, 1995). Notwithstanding that it is consensual that the convergence for a European model of HRM is very unlikely (Brewster, 1995), and the contextualist theories point out a number of factors that distinguish the two models, namely, the greater influence in European countries of the state in organizational life and the greater heterogeneity within and between countries.

Thus, these theories focus not on the relationship between HRM and performance but mainly on the contextual factors that shape HRM models and practices, namely (Brewster et al., 2004; Claus, 2003; Sparrow and Hilthrop, 1997), (1) the environment dimension (international, national, national HRM context—labor legislations and social security provisions, differences in business structure and systems, the degree of state ownership, the fragmentation of industrial sectors) and (2) the organizational dimension (organizational strategy, HRM strategy, HRM practices such as labor relations, organizational communication and development).

It is worth highlighting that the contextualist perspective goes beyond the culturalistic approach, as mentioned by Sparrow and Hilthrop (1997: 215), "(…) if national culture were a primary determinant of HRM one might expect that cultural clusters would each have their own distinctive pattern of overall HRM. This is not so."

Focusing on the relationship between HRM practices and innovation performance, Laursen (2002) emphasizes the sector of activity as an important variable, concluding that more advances in HRM practices, which enable better innovation performance, are more effective and applicable in knowledge-intensive sectors of the economy. Also, Lorenz and Valeyre (2004), based on a research about working conditions in 15 member states of the EU (including Portugal), typified four forms of work organization, namely, learning forms, lean forms, taylorist forms, and traditional forms. The differences in these forms of organization and the differences in HRM practices that are complementary to them (Kovács, 1998) are due to the following factors: sector of activity, firm size, occupational category, and employee demographics (age, sex, and seniority).

In the occupational category, the learning form of organization is especially characteristic of work managers, professionals, and technicians, while the lean form is the most present among blue collar employees, the taylorist form among machine operators and unskilled labor, and the traditional form among the work service workers and market sales person. When firm size is considered, the learning form of work organization is most present in small firms, with 10 to 49 employees, (42.7%), followed by large firms with 500 employees and over (38.7%).

In large firms, the taylorist form and the traditional form of work organization have low representation, with 13.2% (of employees by organizational class) and 15.5%, respectively, with the distribution of work organizational models similar to that of the construction industry.

The analysis of work organizational forms according to employee demographics shows that the learning form is mostly present in firms with older employees (85.5% of employees over 45 years), with higher seniority (43.9% of employees with a seniority of 20 years or more), and in men (40.5%).

Gjerding (1996), in a study about innovation in firms, emphasized the following factors as important for developing innovation: flexible work organization forms; functional flexibility; education and training, especially for top and middle management; and organizational policies.

Within the contextualist perspectives, the "new institutionalism approach" (DiMaggio and Powell, 1983) presents the concept of isomorphism to explain why and how organizations resemble similar organizations in their environment to obtain legitimacy in their markets. There are two types of isomorphism: competitive and institutional.

Competitive isomorphism is linked to a system of rationality that emphasizes market competition, niche change, and fitness measures, whereas institutional isomorphism is an alternative perspective that focuses on three mechanisms of decision making in organizations: coercive mechanisms (change stems from political influence and the problem of legitimacy), mimetic mechanism (change results from standard responses to uncertainty), and normative mechanisms (change stems from professionalization).

In European countries, most HRM practices are introduced by institutional isomorphism, one of the reasons being that the relationship between HRM strategy and the company's strategy is perceived as unclear (Gooderham et al., 2004).

In Portugal, several studies carried out by Marques and Rodrigues (2007) in the construction industry and Marques (2010) and Silva (2013) in technology-intensive firms and knowledge-intensive firms appear to show that most of the practices adopted are by institutional isomorphism, that is, in order to comply with legal (e.g., labor legislation referring to hours of training, health and safety measures) as well as quality certification requirements.

These studies appear to corroborate previous studies carried out by Brandão and Parente (1998) and by Tavares and Caetano (1999) that show the tendency in Portugal for the persistence of personnel management and for practices related to health and safety, thus those that are legally mandatory, as well as the persistence for more traditional work practices that do not require more developed skills.

The third perspective, the resource-based theory, presents itself as an alternative to traditional SHRM. This perspective emphasizes the importance of heterogeneity of internal factors to obtain competitive advantage.

In order to foster competitiveness, internal factors must be, according to Barney (1991), irreplaceable, inimitable, valuable, and rare. The theories included in this perspective can be divided into two groups (Wright and McMahan, 1992): (1) the theories that are centered on the HR of the company, that is, on the "company's human capital pool" and (2) the theories that are centered on HRM practices that are used as instruments to manage this type of resources.

Lepak and Snell's (1999) human capital theory is one of the theories worth mentioning. Crossing two variables, explicitly, the value of human capital with the singularity of human capital, they typified four human capital models: (1) development model (high value and high singularity), an HRM based on the commitment of employees and the promotion of training and career development; (2) acquisition model (high value and low singularity), a model based on mutual gains and on a symbiotic relationship between organization and employee; (3) alliance model (low value and high singularity) based on partnership and collaboration; and (4) contract model (low value and low singularity) based on transactional labor relations that are economically based.

Pichault and Schoenaers (2003) present a more holistic and integrative model. The authors integrate a contingency approach with a political approach and take into consideration the role of organizational actors. They define five HRM models: (1) arbitrary model, centralized on top management (practices are based on the good will of top management; assessment and recruitment is informal, as well as compensations/rewards); (2) codifying model, based on the definition and formalization of HRM criteria to guarantee equal rights, equal pay for equal jobs, and rewards and promotions based on seniority; (3) value model, a volatile model based on the principles of corporate culture; (4) agreement models, a collegial model in which actors participate in the definition of policies and practices; and (5) individualizing model, based on the personalization of labor relationships. Criteria are formalized and integrate both individual and collective practices.

Marques (2010) found a combination of characteristics of the arbitrary model with the characteristics of the development model in family-type SME and the characteristics of the value model combined with the characteristics of the acquisition model in knowledge-intensive firms, whereas in technology-intensive firms linked to the automobile industry with just-in-time the most common models were the combination of codifying model with the contract model.

These models are shaped essentially by the sector of activity and legal and quality certification requirements. The author also found that there is a relationship between the type of HRM model and the job satisfaction of workers, as well as their perception of work. Job satisfaction in general is higher in the value and codifying model and is related to the perception of access to information as well as team work.

Worth mentioning is the role played by work organization models (teamwork enhances the perception of job enrichment and access to information) as well as that of sociodemographic characteristics (level of education and gender).

2.5   Final considerations

Today, Europe is facing a number of economic and social changes that challenge the managing of people at work. The aim of this chapter is to make a brief reflection about some of the factors that shape HRM models in Europe.

Centering our discussion at a macro- and micro-level, we reviewed what we consider some of the key topics in this field, namely, globalization, technological and demographic changes, and the changes in the conceptualization of HRM itself.

At a macro-level, the labor market is under technological pressure that points to a reduction of job posts, but on the other hand, the demographic pressure makes the workers hard to replace, which has reflections in the employment/unemployment rate.

At an organizational level, advances in HRM practices enable better innovation performance and are more effective and applicable in knowledge-intensive sectors of the economy. Some of these practices can include factors as flexible work forms, functional flexibility, education and training, and organizational policies.

As to the latter, we discussed the different perspectives and their impact on understanding this field.

From this reflection we draw as main conclusions that HRM is not only shaped by internal and contextual factors but is embedded in the tensions and ambiguities in these environments, including demographic and technological changes.

References

Alis, D., Horts, C.-H.B., Chevalier, F., Fabi, B., and Peretti, J.-M. *Gestão dos Recursos Humanos—uma abordagem internacional.* Lisboa, Portugal: Edições Piaget, 2014.

António, N.S. *Estratégia Organizacional, do posicionamento ao movimento*, 3ª edição. Lisboa, Portugal: edições Sílabo, 2015.

Arthur, J.B. Effects of human resource systems on manufacturing performance and turnover. *Academy of Management Journal*, 37: 670–687, 1994.

Atkinson, J. Manpower strategies for flexible organizations. *Personnel Management*, 16 (8): 28–31, August 1984.

Barney, J. Firm resources and sustained competitive advantage. *Journal of Management*, 17 (1): 99–120, 1991.

Beardwell, J. and Claydon, T. (eds.). *Human Resource Management—A Contemporary Approach*, 6th edn. Edinburgh, U.K.: Pearson Education Limited, 2010.

Bertrán, J. *Competências Cruciais para Gestores Internacionais*. Lisboa, Portugal: Actual, 2015.

Brandão, A. and Parente, C. Configurações da função pessoal: As especificidades do caso português. *Organizações e Trabalho*, 20: 23–40, 1998.

Brewster, C. Towards a 'European' model of human resource management. *Journal of Business Studies*, First Quarter: 1–21, 1995.

Brewster, C. and Larsen, H.H. *Human Resource Management in Northern Europe, Trends, Dilemmas and Strategy*. Oxford, U.K.: Blackwell Publishers, 2000.

Brewster, C., Wolfgang, M., and Morley, M. (eds.). *Human Resource Management in Europe. Evidence of Convergence?* Amsterdam, The Netherlands: Elsevier Butterworth Hienemann, 2004.

Bruggeman, F., Gazier, B., and Paucard, D. Affronter les restructurations d'entreprise en Europe, propositions pour une démarche unifiée. *La Revue de L'IRES*, 72: 83–118, 2012.

Centeno, M. *O trabalho, uma visão de Mercado*. Lisboa, Portugal: Fundação Francisco Manuel dos Santos, 2013.

Claus, L. Similarities and differences in human resource management in the European Union. *Thunderbird International Business Review*, 45 (6): 729–755, 2003.

Crozier, M. *A Empresa à Escuta*. Lisboa, Portugal: Instituto Piaget, 1994.

da Costa, R.L. *Estratégia Organizacional e "outsourcing": os recursos estratégicos de competitividade empresarial*. Coimbra, Portugal: Almedina, 2012.

Delaney, J.T. and Huselid, M.A. The impact of human resource management practices on perception of organizational performance. *Academy of Management Journal*, 39 (4): 949–969, 1996.

Delery, J.E. and Doty, H.D. Modes of theorizing in strategic Human Resource Management: Tests of Universalistic, Contingency, and configurational Performance Predictions. *Academy of Management Journal*, 39 (4): 802–835, 1996.

Dimaggio, P.J. and Powell, W.W. The iron cage revisited: Institutional isomorphism and collective rationality in organizational fields. In Dimaggio, P.J. and Powell, W.W. (eds.), *The New Institutionalism in Organizational Analysis*. Chicago, IL: The University of Chicago Press, pp. 63–82, 1983.

Edwards, T. and Rees, C. *International Human Resource Management—Globalization, National Systems, and Multinational Companies*. Harlow, U.K.: FT Prentice Hall, 2006.

Giddens, A. *O Mundo na era da Globalização*. Lisboa, Portugal: Editorial Presença, 2000.

Gjerding, A.N. Organisational innovation in the Danish private business sector. DRUID Working Paper 96–16, 1996.

Gooderham, P., Morley, M., Brewster, C., and Mayrhofer, W. Human resource management: A universal concept? In Brewster, C., Wolfgang M., and Morley, M. (eds.), *Human Resource Management in Europe. Evidence of Convergence?*. Oxford, U.K.: Elsevier Butterworth-Heinemann, pp. 3–26, 2004.

Gouveia, L.B., Neves, N., and Carvalho, C. Um ensaio sobre a governação na era da globalização. *Revista Geopolítica*, 3: 235–268, 2009.

Huselid, M.A. The impact of human resource management practices on turnover, productivity, and corporate financial performance. *Academy of Management Journal*, 38 (3): 635–670, 1995.

Instituto Nacional de Estatística (INE). Projeções de população residente 2012–2060. www.ine.pt (consultado a February 25, 2015), 2014.

Keenoy, T. Review article: HRMism and the languages of re-presentation. *Journal of Management Studies*, 34 (5): 825–841, 1997.

Kovács, I. Da controvérsia sobre os novos modelos de produção. In Kovács, I. and Castilho, J. (eds.), *Novos Modelos de Produção*. Oeiras, Portugal: Celta Editora, pp. 5–24, 1998.

Kovács, I. Novas formas de organização do trabalho e autonomia no trabalho. *Sociologia Problemas e Práticas*, 52 (CIES-ISCTE/CELTA), 41–65, 2006.

Legge, K. *Human Resource Management. Rhetoric's and Realities*. New York: Palgrave, 1995.

Lepak, D.P. and Snell, S.A. The human resource architecture: Toward a theory of human capital allocation and development. *Academy of Management Review*, 24 (1): 31–48, 1999.

Lorenz, E. and Valeyre, A. Organizational change in Europe: National models or the diffusion of a new "One Best Way?" DRUID Working paper, April 4, 2004.

Macduffie, J.P. Human resource bundles and manufacturing performance: Organizational logic and flexible production systems in the world auto industry. *Industrial and Labor Relations Review*, 48 (2): 197–221, 1995.

Mahoney, T.A. and Dekop, J.R. Evolution of the concept and practice. *Personnel Administration/Human Resource Management, Yearly Review of Management of the Journal of Management*, 12 (2): 223–241, 1986.

Marques, M.A. *Modelos Organizacionais e Práticas de Gestão de Recursos Humanos: um estudo multi-caso*. Lisboa, Portugal: ISEG-UTL, 2010.

Marques, M.A. and Rodrigues, J. HRM practices in the construction industry in Portugal. In Koufopoulos, D.N. (ed.), *Reflecting on Issues and Controversies in Current Management Trends*. Athens, Greece: ATINER, pp. 131–146, 2007.

Melo, P. and Machado, C. *Gestão de Recursos Humanos nas Pequenas e Médias Empresas—Contextos, Métodos e Aplicações*. Lisboa, Portugal: RH Editora, 2015.

Michelin, F., Levai, I., and Messarovitch, Y. *A Empresa ao serviço dos Homens—E porque não?* Cascais, Portugal: Principia, 2003.

Miles, R.E. and Snow, C.C. Designing strategic human resource systems. *Organizational Dynamics*, 13 (1): 36–52, 1984.

Osterman, P. How common is workplace transformation and who adopts it?. *Industrial and Labor Relations Review*, 47 (2): 173–188, 1994.

Pfeffer, J. *Competitive Advantage through People: Unleashing the Power of the Work Force*. Boston, MA: Harvard Business Review School Press, 1994.

Pfeffer, J. Pitfalls on the road to measurement: The dangerous liaison of human resources with the ideas of Accounting and Finance. *Human Resource Management*, 36 (3): 357–365, 1997.

Pichault, F. and Schoenaers, F. HRM practices in a process of organizational change: A contextualist perspective. *Applied Psychology: An International Review*, 52 (1): 120–143, 2003.

Rego, A. and Cunha, M.P. *Manual de Gestão Transcultural de Recursos Humanos*. Lisboa, Portugal: RH Editora, 2009.

Scott, W.R. and Meyer, J.W. The organization of societal sectors propositions. In Dimaggio, P.J. and W.W. Powell (eds.), *The New Institutionalism in Organizational Analysis*. Chicago, IL: The University of Chicago Press, pp. 108–40, 1983.

Silva, A.R.S. *Formas de Organização de Trabalho nas Empresas TIC. Um Estudo de Caso*. Setubal, Portugal: ESCE, 2013.

Sparrow, P. and Hilthrop, J.-M. Redefining the field of European human resource management: A battle between national mindsets and forces of business transition? *Human Resource Management*, 36 (2): 201–219, 1997.

Storey, J. Introduction: From personnel management to human resource management. In Storey, J. (ed.), *New Perspective on Human Resource Management*. London, U.K.: Routledge, pp. 1–18, 1995.

Tavares, S. and Caetano, A. A emergência da gestão de recursos humanos estratégica. In Caetano, A. (coord.), *Mudança Organizacional e Gestão de Recursos Humanos*. Lisboa, Portugal: OEFP, 1999.

Torrington, D. Human resource management and the personnel function. In Storey, J. (ed.). New *Perspective on Human Resource Management*. London, U.K.: Routledge, pp. 56–66, 1995.

Veloso, A. and Keating, J. Gestão de Recursos Humanos em PME's de elevada tecnologia. *Psicologia*, XXII (1): 35–58, 2008.

Walton, R.E. From control to commitment in the workplace. *Harvard Business Review*, 63 (March–April): 77–84, 1985.

Wood, S.J. Human resource management and performance. *International Journal of Management Reviews*, 4 (1): 367–413, 1999.

Wright, P.M. and McMahan, G.C. Theoretical perspectives for strategic human resource management. *Journal of Management*, 18 (2): 295–320, 1992.

chapter three

The concept of e-HRM, its evolution and effects on organizational outcomes

Mine Afacan Findikli and Yasin Rofcanin

Contents

Abstract

Transition of today's work setting has placed human resource management (HRM) practices in the central position. Coupled with changes in technology and information system developments, the nature of HRM practices has also adapted to such developments. Building on these recent trends, the aim of this chapter is to elaborate the field of electronic HRM (e-HRM) in research. We systematically examine the definition of e-HRM and conceptualize its relationship with organizational outcomes. Increasing prevalence of e-HRM carries important theoretical and practical implications for managers as well as researchers. We end our chapter with future research avenues.

Keywords: Electronic HRM, strategic HRM

3.1   Transition from HRM into SHRM

The early 1980s witnessed the growth of "human resource management" (HRM) portraying a new form involving certain practices such as regulation procedures and applying strategies of the upper management. Nonetheless, considering the input of human resource as an important factor for the attainment of competition power and continuation of organizational performance/success, the significance and the functioning of HRM in organization have substantially increased. In this view, since the early 2000s, HRM has evolved into a management style, called "strategic human resource management" (SHRM). Its main focus is to develop ability, knowledge, and creativity and to meet the needs/demands of employees. Due to its swift adaptation capability to changing environmental conditions, SHRM is also considered to be an important support system for the representativeness of the employees and for organizational success. While SHRM contributes to the preparation of the institutional environment in which the development and improvement of employee output are formed, it also acts as a strategic partner for the formation of targeted values.

Taking into account these points, Huselid, Jackson, and Schuler (1997: 171) explained the strategic human resource practices as the formation and execution of a set of internally reliable policies and practices aiming to accomplish the targeted outputs of organization and to achieve the company targets and supply the human capital. In that respect, the main role of SHRM practices can be identified as the attainment of efficient and effective benefits from the organizations' knowledge and human resource capabilities.

Parallel to the new technological developments, the SHRM started adapting itself to these fast changes. Organizations that have been in swift transformation and adaptation processes from industrial to informational age (Ensher, Nielson, & Grant-Vallone, 2002) are rearranging their work flow processes with the effective utilization of technology. These developments, in turn, necessitate certain structural modification including a change from physical to information technology, capital-centred to human-centred economy, and conflict to cooperative working relationships (Nenwani & Raj, 2013: 423). In this framework, the Internet and technology usage became indispensable for the SHRM as much as for the overall functioning of organizations. For this reason, electronic human resource management (e-HRM) has emerged to be a driving force behind HRM value creation (Ruël & Kaap, 2012).

In parallel to the developments in information technologies, the e-HRM has become a highly debated subject and received substantial scholarly attention since its early introduction in 1995 (Strohmeier, 2007). The six fundamental triggering factors for the formation of e-HRM (Jones, 1997: 5–6) are summarized here:

Information technology: It has become essential for e-HRM to adapt to fast changes in computer software, hardware, and networks so that work processes on human resources become effective.

Reengineering of processes: Human resource managers redesign business processes and enhance functioning and the overall productivity of the organization.

Swift management: Organizations are required to work skillfully and swiftly in order to compete with competition. For this particular reason, the e-HRM practices are believed to reduce the overall costs of business processes.

Network organizations: Organizations are in search of less bureaucratic and more practical solutions. With the use of information technology provided by local area networks, e-mails, and mutual intranet, information can be easily transferred among coworkers and stakeholders, hence enabling more effective use of human resources.

Information workers: With the use of information technologies, employees can swiftly gather, form, reform, and use valuable information that in turn allow the organization to learn and put forward new work opportunities.

Globalization: All organizations are required to develop global working strategies in order to compete in the twenty-first century. In other words, human resource departments should be restructured in order to meet the needs/demands of employees.

3.2   What is e-HRM?

Integration of computers in work life along with the rapid changes in Internet technologies influenced HRM, which in turn, transformed this management system into e-HRM. As a matter of fact, the concept of e-HRM originated from e-trade (Ruël, Bondarouk, & Looise, 2004), yet the concept of e-HRM is generally used to describe the administration of human resource practices with the help of the Internet, intranet, and networks.

Before delving into the e-HRM concept, it is important to identify and define its related concepts. In the literature, in addition to e-HRM, there are various terms such as virtual HRM (e.g., Lepak & Snell, 1998), web-based HRM, business-to-employee (B2E) (e.g., Huang, Jin, & Yang, 2004), computer-based human resource management systems (CHRIS) (Ruël et al., 2004; Strohmeier, 2007), and HRIS (Chugh, 2014) that are used for the same phenomenon. Accordingly, "virtual HRM" refers to technological arbitrated networks of diverse internal and external actors providing the organizations with the HR services required for the advancement of conventional HR departments. Through this process, these HRM practices become "virtual." Differently, e-HRM is considered to be receptive of the less developed variety of technology applications such as shared performance of an application process by a conventional HR department and an applicant via the Internet. "Web-based HRM," on the other hand, combines this concept to Internet technologies. e-HRM is also predominantly web orientated and involves supplementary technologies like networked ERP-systems. In a similar vein, the concept of "business-to-employee" condenses the phenomenon to the internal actor categories of "business" (supposedly line managers and HR professionals) and "employees." In contrast, e-HRM involves relevant actor categories such as applicants or consultants (Strohmeier, 2007: 20). From a different lens, computer-based human resource management systems (CHRIS) consists of "a fully integrated, organization-wide network of HR-related data, information, services, databases, tools and transactions." CHRIS therefore can be depicted as a form of e-HRM, involving the application of conventional, web, and voice technologies in order to provide a substantive advancement to the HR administration, transactions, and process performance (Nenwai & Raj, 2013: 422).

In sum, it can be argued that all the aforementioned concepts are related to the main characteristics of e-HRM, but they are usually referred to as the limited version of it (Strohmeier, 2007: 20). It can also be argued that the development of web-based technologies has contributed to the adoption of a new strategic organizational role following the liberation of HR functions from previous restrictions such as time- and energy-consuming processes including benefits and payroll (Ashbaugh & Rowan, 2002).

Literature offers important and distinctive definitions of e-HRM. For instance, Karakanian (2002) defines e-HRM as "the overall HR strategy that lifts HR, shifts it from the HR Department and isolated HR activities, and redistributes it to the organisation and its trusted business partners old and new." In a similar vein, Ruël et al. (2004) describe e-HRM as a method of implementation of various HRM strategy, policy, and practices within organizations by means of mindful and direct support and use of web-based technology channels. Furthermore, Ernst Biesalski states that "Electronic-Human Resource Management (E-HRM) is a web based tool to automate and support HR processes." As emphasized by Kauffman, "An automation system is a precisely planned change in a physical or administrative task utilizing a new process, method, or machine that increases productivity, quality and profit while providing methodological control and analysis. The value of system automation is in its ability to improve efficiency; reduce wasted resources associated with rejects or errors; increase consistency, quality and customer satisfaction; and maximize profit" (Kaur, 2013: 36).

e-HRM can also be distinguished as the (planning, provision, implementation, and operation) application of information technology for supporting and networking at least two (individual and/or collective) actors in their shared performance of HR tasks (Strohmeier, 2007). In a similar vein, Hooi (2006) argues that e-HRM essentially unites and connects employees and managers with the HR department electronically through the HR portal, and e-HRM provides direct access for employees to information systems via the Internet. This approach of e-HRM, in turn, enables all employees and stakeholders to be involved in the business processes electronically that in turn allows people to work easily without being subject to environmental restrictions (p. 466). Marler and Fisher (2010) proposed a hybrid definition on e-HRM as "e-HRM consists of intended and actual HRM policies, activities, services, and collaborations with individuals and organizations, which are delivered and enabled using configurations of computer hardware, software, and electronic networking capability."

In the light of the aforementioned descriptions, Bondarouk and Ruël provide a comprehensive definition of e-HRM. According to them (2009: 507), e-HRM is "An umbrella term covering all possible integration mechanisms & contents between HRM & Information Technologies aiming at creating value within & across organizations for targeted employees & management." In sum, concerning e-HRM, it is generally observed that the functions of the human resource departments within organizations are to a great extent moved to the web environment. Expectedly, e-HRM systems contribute to the simplification and reformation of various HR processes such as job analysis, recruitment, selection, training, compensation, performance management, and HR planning (Stone & Dulebohn, 2013).

3.3   Theoretical perspectives of e-HRM

Studies on the theoretical framework of e-HRM focus on diverging approaches including the sociotechnical systems theory, contingency theory, coordination theory, actor–network theory, and improvisation theory;

and these theories are commonly analyzed within two main dimensions. According to Bondarouk (2011: 7), the first dimension deals with the relative significance of "prescriptive" versus "enacted" e-HRM implementation, whereas the second dimension tackles the extent to which an e-HRM application is accepted as a "tangible" physical system versus "mental framework: linear and dynamic approaches in e-HRM."

Marler and Fisher (2010) also indicate that there are relevant theoretical foundations in strategy, information sciences, and strategic HRM literatures. According to them, the crucial theories in the strategy research in relation to the e-HRM and strategic HR relationship include the contingency theory, the resource-based view (RBV), and strategic evolution, value chain theories, and institutional theory, whereas information science theories involve technological determinism, structuration theory, innovation diffusion theories, technology acceptance theories, and information processing theory.

A closer look at the literature (e.g., Maler & Fisher, 2013; Ruël & Kaap, 2012; Ruel et al., 2007; Strohmeier, 2007) reveals that there is still no grand or integrative multilevel theory of e-HRM. It can be observed that the major theoretical framework of these studies emerges as the contingency theory. However, Strohmeier (2007), in his study, discards these assumptions and instead adopts a different approach to classify contextual factors in the micro and macro level. Nonetheless, the contingency theory could be usefully interpreted within e-HRM. On the other hand, the second crucial theory can be identified as the RBV; the third one as the transaction cost theory; and the last one as the new institutional theory.

Lawrence and Lorch's (1967) contingency theory stipulates that organizations are heavily influenced by their environment. Therefore, the success of the organization depends on the extent to which it shapes its internal structuring by taking into account the limitations imposed by their environment (Lawrence & Lorch, 1967). Even though the propositions of the contingency theory are limited to the organization and its environment, there is a clear necessity to analyse the HRM issues in context (Jackson & Shuller, 1995). It is highly visible implicitly or explicitly that the management information systems (MIS) of the HRM directly benefit from the perspective of the contingency theory. A closer elaboration of the list of variables that Weill and Olson (1987) use in their study fits well with the variables that are most widely used by the contingency theory, namely, strategy, structure, size, environment, technology, individual, and task. These variables are assumed to influence the design, management, actual use, and implementation of the MIS. Based on these assumptions, it can be hypothesized that the higher the "fit" between these variables, the better will be the performance of the IS. The "fit" here is defined as a situation where factors or variables are positioned in such a way that the ideal situation or outcome is obtained (Ruël & Kaap, 2012: 265).

Similar to Strohmeier's categorization of micro and macro level of e-HRM, Ruël and Kaap (2012: 267) classified the e-HRM variables as follows:

3.4   Context variables in e-HRM research and theoretical frameworks

Micro	Macro
Support from colleagues and managers	Organization size
Information availability and	Department size
accessibility of HRM practices	Duration of existence of HRIS
Employee skills	department
Employee behavior	Computer experience of the firm
Computer and Internet literacy	Cross-functional teams
Personal characteristics of individuals	Nationality of the firm
Characteristics of the technology	Multicultural context
Degree of involvement in e-HRM	National culture
design and implementation	
Managerial compulsion to use e-HRM	
Privacy and data security	

3.4.1   Resource-based view theory

The RBV contents that human resources are the most valuable resources of companies in gaining competitive advantage as they are valuable, unique, inimitable, and imperfectly substitutable (Barney, 1991). Following this approach, companies have sought to develop the best system that would allow them to use in the most effective way the knowledge, skills, and competences they have. Therefore, e-HRM practices such as e-recruiting, e-learning, etc., can be seen as activities that help the firm to meet these objectives. When unique and inimitable characteristics of human resources are considered, different e-HRM practices are likely to create significant imbalances among the competing companies. Such e-HRM activities are particularly helpful in diminishing costs and accelerating the processes that are likely to make HR activities more effective. This proposition is found to be highly consistent with Ruël et al.'s (2004) finding that e-HRM aims to generate efficiency gains or reduce costs by cutting headcounts or removing administration. Indeed, as Parry (2011: 9) has demonstrated, a number of authors (e.g., Ensher et al., 2002; Lengnick-Hall & Moritz, 2003; Martin et al., 2008; Snell et al., 2002) have supported this assertion. Besides, 67% of companies confirmed that the use of technology has contributed to the improvement of their organizational efficiency, while 70% of them reported progress in the quality and timeliness of human resource services to their employees (Bell, Lee, & Yeung, 2006).

3.4.2   Transaction cost theory

The transaction cost theory presupposes that the institutional arrangements are cost-effective. According to this theory, e-HRM structures that are compound, partially subcontracted, dispersed, or delegated are found to be competent on saving costs (Lepak & Snell, 1998). As a matter of fact, studies on transaction cost theory show that by using technology, the human resource transaction costs can be reduced by 75% and costs associated with the technology can be regained in less than 2 years (Bell et al., 2006). For instance, information system networks that were created with the e-HRM use websites and social media and can reach more candidates compared to the traditional methods, thereby reducing the transaction costs significantly compared to the traditional methods.

Besides, information and communication technology (ICT) entails a more effective training by using distant training tools and interactive learning methods. The basic facilities established with e-HRM activities simplify and accelerate performance rating, pricing, and related activities compared to traditional methods and allow rapid transfer of recorded information to the decision support systems (Andersen & Fagerhaug, 2002; Armstrong, 2006). Therefore, for the transaction cost theory, IT is considered not only as the technological but also as the economical enabler of e-HRM.

3.4.3   New institutional theory

Institutional theory is widely used to explain HRM practices and the factors that influence them (Heikkilä, 2013). According to this theory, regardless of their relevance to actual performance accomplishment, organizations should pay attention to the institutional expectations of their environment in addition to responding to the market pressures. Therefore, any change in the organizations can be explained by the pressures from public agencies, expectations of the society, as well as the actions of the leading organizations; and e-HRM may be postulated as such a change. As the value and efficiency of IT institutions are rarely questioned, there is a potential pressure on organizations to adopt such practices as e-recruiting or e-learning, whether the traditional methods satisfy organizational needs or not. Therefore, e-HRM is generally treated as a means of gaining legitimacy for HRM and the entire organization. From this perspective, the institutionalist approaches provide us with a deeper understanding of the actual performance contributions of the e-HRM.

On the other hand, the institutional theory also envisages the isomorphism of resulting configurations, since coercive and normative and mimetic mechanisms will lead to isomorphic configurations. By and large, institutionalism proposes explanations of the relation between institutional context and configurations of e-HRM while putting forward a critical view on its factual consequences (Strohmeier, 2007: 29).

3.5   Types of e-HRM

The literature review provides us some clear-cut categorizations of the HRM activities. The first categorization is presented by Wright and Dyer (2000) who based their analysis on face-to-face communication and online services and identified e-HRM's roles in the organizations as transactional HRM, traditional HRM, and transformational HRM. In a similar vein, Lepak and Snell (1998) classified them as operational, relational, and transformational HRMs. Operational HRM refers to the basic HRM activities in the administrative area such as salary administration (payroll) and personal data administration. Relational HRM focuses on more advanced HRM activities that are at the core of business processes such as recruiting and the selection of new personnel, training, performance management and appraisal, and rewards. Transformational HRM, on the other hand, adopts a strategic dimension and works on activities such as organizational change processes, strategic orientation, strategic competence management, and strategic knowledge management. Finally, it should be underlined that in terms of transformational HRM, it is possible to create a workforce that is open to change in line with the company's strategic choices by using web-based or paper-based materials (Ruël et al., 2004).

Furthermore, Strohmeier and Kabst (2014) provide another comprehensive categorization of the e-HRM activities and find that the first classification based on the criterion of information system function works as an automational and informational type. It is concluded that activities that are named as "automational e-HRM" help support administration by trying to reduce costs and increase efficiency. It is further observed that informational e-HRM activities go beyond the automation provided by technology and aim at supporting the decision-making process of HRM activities and increasing their quality.

Researchers convey that the second categorization is based on the corporate importance of the e-HRM and therefore has two subdimensions identified as operative and strategic. Operative e-HRM shows a "nonstrategic" characteristic while supporting the firm by improving efficiency, costs, and velocity of e-HRM via the electronic support of administrative tasks. Strategic e-HRM activities, on the other hand, support e-HRM especially by contributing to firm performance. Finally, a third classification based on the objectives of e-HRM distinguishes e-HRM as operational, relational, and transformational. Operational e-HRM objectives improve the effectiveness and efficiency of HRM by the automation and support possibilities. Relational e-HRM objectives are aimed at improving the stakeholder relations and service delivery of e-HRM and are concerned with the supportive business process by means of training, recruitment, and performance management. Last, transformational e-HRM objectives signify the developments in the business support and strategy orientation of e-HRM such as knowledge management and strategic reorientation (Nivlouei, 2014; Strohmeier & Kabst, 2014).

3.6   e-HRM goals

Building on the study of Lepak and Snell (1998) and based on the case study of five large international organizations, Ruël et al. (2004) identified three types of goals for organizations as a result of e-HRM usage. These steps improve the strategic orientation of e-HRM, cost reduction/ efficiency gains, and client service improvement/facilitating management and employees. Moreover, Bondarouk and her colleagues added a fourth objective, which allows for the integration of HR functions (of different organizational units or entire organizations). On the other hand, Nenwani and Raj (2013) put forward a new e-HRM objective by also reemphasizing the objectives in previous studies. According to them (Nenwani and Raj, 2013: 424), the following applies:

- Improving the series to HR department clients including employees and management.
- Increasing efficiency and reducing costs while accelerating different processes and making HR become a strategic partner in achieving organizational goals.
- Providing access to HR information and connecting all parts of the company and external organizations that eventually help share information and build teams.
- Allowing standardization that ensures that an organization remains compliant with HR requirements while warranting a more precise decision making.
- Assisting HR with transactional and transformational goals. While the former helps to reduce costs, the latter helps the allocation of time improvement for HR professionals so that they may address more strategic issues.

Last, it appears that Kaur (2013: 37) has identified six objectives of e-HRM.

In light of this information, with the use of technological tools and application, it can be argued that e-HRM activities are not only a strategic partner of the top management but also the agents of change due to their ability to (1) cultivate an organizational culture open to continuous learning, innovation, and development; (2) maintain transparency in knowledge, learning, evolution, career, and rewarding policies; (3) ensure a multidimensional organizational communication; and (4) reduce the costs in business processes and support the decision-making process by facilitating the access to information.

3.7 e-HRM outcomes

Researchers have reached to general understandings and conclusions based on the outcomes of the e-HRM activities. For instance, Marler and Fisher (2010) argue that HRM investments help reduce the costs by restructuring HRM operations, advancing efficiency by improving the quality of HRM services, and transforming HRM functions to a strategic business partner. HRM's influence on the efficiency and effectiveness of HRM activities is well captured by Kaur (2013: 37) through reduction of the paper work by increasing data precision and also by reducing excess HRM while preserving the quality of HRM's data. Additionally, because e-HRM provides easy access to HR data and facilitates classifying and reclassifying of data, it also entails a more transparent system. Furthermore, it can be deducted that e-HRM facilitates a more positive organizational culture through a higher internal profile for HR. Among the other advantages are the integral support it provided for the management of human resources and other basic support processes within the company decentralizing the HR tasks.

On the other hand, Ruël and Kapp (2012) identify e-HRM outcomes within the framework of value creation as efficiency, effectiveness, or service quality. Similarly, Nivlouei (2014: 151) expresses e-HRM outcomes in her work as (1) high workforce commitment, (2) high competence, (3) cost-effectiveness, and (4) higher congruence. Strohmeier (2007: 21) identifies e-HRM outcomes within the framework of the micro and macro levels. While the micro-level outcomes focus on individual impacts such as user satisfaction or acceptance, macro-level outcomes are classified as operational, relational, and/or transformational. Operational outcomes are related to the efficiency and effectiveness outcomes of e-HRM like cost reduction or lightening administrative workload. Relational outcomes refer to the interaction and network of different actors. The transformational outcomes are motivated by fundamental reorientations of the general scope and the function of HRM that include the capability to contribute to the overall performance of the organization. Thus, the integration of Internet technologies into the HRM processes provided the minimization of costs in all functions of HRM including planning, recruitment, learning and training, performance appraisal, career planning, salary system, industrial relations, and health and safety systems.

3.8   e-HRM functions

3.8.1   Electronic human resource planning

e-HRM systems offer mechanisms that facilitate the collection, restoration, and update of the existing data related to the knowledge, skills, and competences of the organization's employees and access to the data when required. This provides a faster and much more knowledgeable decision-making process should new initiatives are demanded by other departments within the organization (Hopkins & Markham, 2003: 57–58).

3.8.2   Electronic recruitment

Reducing the costs of recruitment and speeding up the process and access to a much broader job application pool are among the contributions of the use of the Internet in recruitment. These advantages of the use of the Internet increased the popularity of electronic recruitment among the human resource experts working in different sectors and expanded the use of electronic recruitment (Pearce & Tuten, 2001: 9). Technology is used not only in recruiting candidates to the organizations but also in selecting work activities for these candidates (Hogler, Henle, & Bemus, 1998: 152). Thus, it helps to provide a larger candidate pool and more effective recruitment process due to the shortening of the process and reducing of the costs of recruitment (Marchington & Wilkinson, 2005: 174).

3.8.3   e-Learning

e-Learning can be depicted as a new innovative approach providing a well-designed, student-oriented, interactive, and facilitated learning environment for anyone at any place and time by utilizing open and flexible learning materials and various digital technological resources and properties (Khan, 2005: 3). e-Learning is also defined by the American Society for Training and Development (ASTD) as a wide range of activities and processes such as Internet-based learning, computer-based learning, online classes, and digital collaborations (Derouin, Fritzsche, & Salas, 2005: 920).

3.8.4   Electronic performance management

Electronic performance management can be connoted as the use of audiovisual computer systems for the collection, storage, analysis, and reporting of performance data of an individual and/or group (Phillips, Isenhour, & Stone, 2008: 199–200). The main objective of the use of technology in performance rating is to develop individual performances and thus the organization's performance by providing the employees with the necessary knowledge, techniques, and methods as well as the support systems (Benson, Johnson, & Kuchinke, 2002: 398).

3.8.5   Electronic career management

Computer-based career guidance systems are diagnostic tools that identify and put across the priorities required for the development of employees. Additionally, these systems provide the employees with the facilities to compare the knowledge and skills they hold with the skills and competences required at the present and future positions (Rothwell, Jackson, Knight, & Lindholm, 2005: 122–124).

3.8.6   e-Compensation

With e-compensation, managers can design, manage, and report compensation policies in a more effective way by using web-based software tools (Dulebohn & Marler, 2005: 167). Additionally, they are able to administer routine compensation management duties such as responding to the employees, should they ask for information on their confidential information or specific rewarding systems (Wolf, 2000: 183–184). e-Compensation tools facilitate the conduct of bureaucratic duties by the flow of real-time data and knowledge. Besides, electronic charging can be benefited in the maintenance of wage equality (Dulebohn & Marler, 2005: 166–167).

3.8.7   Electronic industrial relations

Web-based software facilitates the establishment of a system that helps managers in their decision making on the potential problems in the area of industrial relations. These systems are necessary for the bargaining of collective labor contract and useful for the presentation of variables that are hard to obtain such as the data on the absenteeism of employees, overtime work/labor shift, the information on shifts, and the impact on costs (Ashbaugh & Miranda, 2002: 16).

3.8.8   Electronic occupational safety and health

Managers are continuously informed about the effectiveness of the activities aimed at reducing the risks of accidents through reports prepared on occupational diseases, accidents, and disabilities and encourage replanning of the works and processes that take into consideration the risk of accidents. Additionally, employees might be informed electronically about the specific risks that they might face in the form of personalized information; thus, it might be possible to change the attitudes of the employees without mediation of an expert.

References

Andersen, B., & Fagerhaug, T. (2002). *Performance Measurement Explained: Designing and Implementing Your State-of-the-Art System*. Milwaukee, WI: The American Society for Quality.

Armstrong, M. (2006). *A Handbook of Human Resource Management Practice* (10th ed.). London, U.K.: Kogan Page Limited.

Ashbaugh, S., & Miranda, R. (2002). Technology for human resources management: Seven questions and answers. *Public Personnel Management*, 31(1), 7–20.

Barney, J. B. (1991). Firm resources and sustained competitive advantage. *Journal of Management*, 17(1), 99–120.

Bell, B. S., Lee, S. -W., & Yeung, S. K. (2006). The impact of eHR on professional competence in HRM: Implications for the development of HR professionals. CAHRS Working Paper Series. Retrieved from http://digitalcommons. ilr.cornell.edu/cahrswp/403, accessed May 12, 2015.

Benson, A. D., Johnson, S. D., & Kuchinke, K. P. (2002). The use of technology in the digital workplace: A framework for human resource development. *Advances in Developing Human Resources*, C:IV(4), 392–404.

Bondarouk, T. (2011). Theoretical approaches to e-HRM implementations. In T. Bondarouk, H. Ruël, & J. C. Looise (Eds.), *Electronic HRM in Theory and Practice*. London, U.K.: Emerald Group Publishing Limited.

Bondarouk, T., & Ruel, H. (2009). Electronic human resource management: Challenges in the digital era. *The International Journal of Human Resource Management*, 20(3), 505–514.

Chugh, R. (2014). Role of human resource information systems in an educational organization. *Journal of Advanced Management Science*, 2(2), 149–153.

Derouin, R. E., Fritzsche, B. A., & Salas, E. (2005). E-learning in organizations. *Journal of Management*, C:XXXI(6), 920–940.

Dulebohn, J. H., & Marler, J. H. (2005). E-compensation: The potential to transform practice?. In H. G. Gueutal & D. L. Stone (Eds.), *The Brave New World of eHR: Human Resources Management in the Digital Age*. San Francisco, CA: John Wiley & Sons, Inc., pp. 166–189.

Ensher, E. A., Nielson, T. R., & Grant-Vallone, E. (2002). Tales from the hiring line: Effects of the internet and technology on HR processes. *Organizational Dynamics*, 31(3), 222–244.

Heikkilä, J. -P. (2013). An institutional theory perspective on e-HRM's strategic potential in MNC subsidiaries. *Journal of Strategic Information Systems*, 22, 238–251.

Hogler, R. L., Henle, C., & Bemus, C. (1998). Internet recruiting and employment discrimination: A legal perspective. *Human Resource Management Review*, C:VIII(2), 149–164.

Hooi, L. W. (2006). Implementing e-HRM: The readiness of small and medium sized manufacturing companies in Malaysia. *Asia Pacific Business Review*, 12(4), 465–485.

Hopkins, B., & Markham, J. (2003). *e-HR: Using Intranets to Improve the Effectiveness of Your People*. Hampshire, U.K.: Gower Publishing Limited.

Huang, J. -H., Jin, B. -H., & Yang, C. (2004). Satisfaction with business-to-employee benefit systems and organizational citizenship behavior: An examination of gender differences. *International Journal of Manpower*, 25(2), 195–210.

Huselid, M. A., Jackson, S. E., & Schuler, R. S. (1997). Technical and strategic human resource management effectiveness as determinants of firm performance. *The Academy of Management Journal*, 40(1), 171–188.

Jackson, S. & Schuler, R.S. (1995). Understanding human resource management in the context of organizational environments. In N.R. Rosen Zurig & L.W. Porter (Eds.), *Annual Review of Psychology*, 46, 29–37.

Jones, J. W. (1997). *Virtual HR: Human Resources Management in the Information Age*. Menlo Park, CA: Crisp Publications.

Karakanian, M. (2002). *Are Human Resource Departments Ready for e-HR*. In S. Purba (Ed.), *Architectures for E-business System Building. The Foundation for Tomorrow's Success*. London, U.K.: Auerbach Publications.

Kaur, P. (2013). E-HRM: A boon or bane?, Anveshanam. *A National Journal of Management*, 1(1), 35–38 [August 2012–July 2013].

Khan, B. H. (2005). *Managing e-Learning: Design, Delivery, Implementation and Evaluation*. London, U.K.: Information Science Publishing.

Lawrence, P. R., & Lorsch, J. W. (1967). Differentiation and integration in complex organizations. *Administrative Science Quarterly*, 12(1), 1–47.

Lengnick-Hall M. & Moritz S. (2003). The impact of e-HR on the human resource management function. *Journal of Labor Research*, 24(3), 365–379.

Lepak, D. P., & Snell, S. A. (1998). Virtual HR: Strategic human resource management in the 21st century. *Human Resource Management Review*, 8(3), 215–234.

Marchington, M., & Wilkinson, A. (2005). *Human Resource Management at Work: People Management and Development*, 3rd edn. London, U.K.: Chartered Institute of Personnel & Development (CIPD) Publishing.

Marler, J. H., & Fisher, S. L. (2010). An evidence-based review of E-HRM and strategic human resource management. *Third European Academic Workshop on Electronic Human Resource Management Proceedings*, pp. 33–51, New York.

Marler, J.H., & Fisher, S.L. (2013). An evidence-based review of e-HRM and strategic human resource management review, 23, 18–36.

Martin G., Redddington M. & Alexander H. (2008). Technology, outsourcing and transforming HR. Oxford, U.K.: Elsevier.

Nenwani, P. J., & Raj, M. D. (2013). E-HRM prospective in present scenario. *International Journal of Advance Research in Computer Science and Management Studies*, 1(7), 422–428.

Nivlouei, F. B. (2014). Electronic human resource management system: The main element in capacitating globalization paradigm. *International Journal of Business and Social Science*, 5(2), 147–159.

Parry, E. (2011). An examination of e-HRM as a means to increase the value of the HR function. *The International Journal of Human Resource Management*, 22(5), 1146–1162.

Pearce, C. G., & Tuten, T. L. (2001). Internet recruiting in the banking industry. *Business Communication Quarterly*, C:LXIV(1), 9–18.

Phillips, T. N., Isenhour, L. C., & Stone, D. (2008). The potential for privacy violations in electronic human resource practices. In G. Martin, M. Reddington, & H. Alexander (Eds.), *Technology, Outsourcing & Transforming HR*. Burlington, MA: Elsevier Ltd., pp. 193–230.

Rothwell, W. J., Jackson, R. D., Knight, S., & Lindholm, J. (2005). *Career Planning and Succession Management: Developing Your Organization's Talent-for Today and Tomorrow*. Santa Barbara, CA: Greenwood Publishing Group, Inc.

Ruël, H., Bondarouk, T., & Looise, J. K. (2004). e-HRM: Innovation or irritation: An explorative empirical study in five large companies on Web-based HRM. *Management Revue*, 15(3), 364–380.

Ruël, H., Bondarouk, T. & Van der Velde, M. (2007). The contribution of e-HRM to HRM effectiveness. *Employee Relations*, 29(3), 280–291.

Ruël, H., & Kaap, van der H. (2012). E-HRM usage and value creation. Does a facilitating context matter? *German Journal of Research in Human Resource Management*, 26(3), 260–281.

Schuler, R. S., & Jackson, S. E. (1987). Linking competitive strategies with human resource practices. *Academy of Management*, 1(3), 207–219.

Snell, S., Stueber, D., & Lepak, D. (2002). Virtual HR departments: getting out of the middle. In R. Henneman, D. Greenberger (Eds.), *Human Resource Management in Vitual Organizations*, Greenwich: Information Age Publishing.

Stone, D. L., & Dulebohn, J. H. (2013). Emerging issues in theory and research on electronic human resource management (eHRM). *Human Resource Management Review*, 23, 1–5.

Strohmeier, S. (2007). Research in e-HRM: Review and implications. *Human Resource Management Review*, 17(1), 19–37.

Strohmeier, S. (2009). Concepts of e-HRM consequences: a categorisation, review and suggestion. *International Journal of Human Resource Management*, 20(3), 528–543.

Weill, P., & Olson, M. (1987). An assessment of the contingency theory of MIS. Working Paper IS-87-31. Department of Information Systems, New York University.

Wolf, M. G. (2000). Computers and compensation administration. In L. A. Berger & D. R. Berger (Eds.), *The Compensation Handbook: A State-of-the-Art Guide to Compensation Strategy and Design*, 4th edn. New York: The McGraw-Hill Companies, Inc., pp. 183–188.

Wright, P., & Dyer, L. (2000). People in the e-business: New challenges, new solutions. Working paper 00-11, Center for Advanced Human Resource Studies, Cornell University, Ithaca, New York.

chapter four

Organizational change success as a communicational agency effect
Structuration, textualizing, and networking

Ivo Manuel Pontes Domingues

Contents

Abstract

This study intends to analyze the decisive importance of internal organizational communication to the success of an extraordinary organizational change that was undertaken in a factory owned by a multinational group. This rapid, deep, and wide change was based on the implementation of management methods, which reinforces both the importance of the relationship between human and nonhuman agencies and the importance of communicational agency. The theoretical framework offers an eclectic and multitheoretical approach that is based on the structuration theory, actor–network theory, and co-orientation theory, which permits to understand the importance of communication agency in the complex processes of change.

Keywords: Agency, authority, responsibility, empowerment, resources, technologies, management method

4.1 Introduction

The literature on organizational change considers organizational communication. However, tendentiously, organizational communication is regarded as a process that supports and enables change, but this literature does not sufficiently consider the relationship between communication and performance, because it provides a limited connection between communication processes and other organizational processes. Hence, the present study intends to analyze communication based on a different theoretical and empirical approach. Concretely, the perspective employed in the present analysis is based on the following assumptions: Ontologically, organizational change is a social, organizational, technological, and communicational construction, and communication is both a context-dependent process and an agentic performance of human and nonhuman actants; epistemologically, organizational change is both a cause and an effect of communication, and communication can be understood as both an inducer and an amplifier of organizational change; methodologically, organizational change can be analyzed as the practical use of codes to inform and share data, and meanings and communication can be addressed using constructivist methods.

To analyze organizational communication, I adopted a theoretical framework of analysis that integrates concepts borrowed from the structuration theory (ST), actor–network theory (ANT), and co-orientation theory (CT). Beyond their focus on signification and communication, these theories possess epistemological commensurability, as they deny the macro–micro dichotomy and the structure–agency dichotomy (Giddens, 1979: 76–79; 1984: 139–144; Latour, 2005a: 202–220; Law, 1994: 56–62; Taylor and Van Every, 2000: 143, 154; 2011: 244). Beyond this epistemological commensurability, they also share a focus on communication issues and represent the most recent and systematized ways to analyze communication associated with change.

ST contributes to the analysis of (re)production signification, which is fundamental to the analysis of changes in meaning that support effective change in organizational processes. ANT contributes to the analysis of communication performed by human and nonhuman actants, which is very helpful for understanding central change processes, such as mechanization and informatization. CT contributes to the analysis of nonhuman agency based on texts, which are essential to define, orient, and legitimate organizational changes. In contrast to ANT and CT, ST does not account for organizational phenomena, but its inclusion in the theoretical framework is fully justifiable because it provides a framework for the conceptualization of agency in the other theories and provides a dedicated theory for structural (re)production, which can be applied to the analysis of organizational issues, and there are many organizational studies rooted in its conceptualization of the signification dimension of communication. To the best of my knowledge, such a theoretical triangulation has never been performed, as I reviewed 129 journals that were included in the "Social Science Citation Index," up to the year 2014, and focused on one or more of the relevant research issues (organizational, management, innovation, change, business, and communication). No papers provided an analytical comparison of the explanatory capacity of these theories.

This reflection aims (1) to understand the role of communication in a deep, quick, and wide organizational change undertaken in a threatening external and internal environment, on which organizational survival depends; (2) to understand the relationships between changes to production processes and changes to communication processes, which are mediated by management models; and (3) to validate this theoretical triangulation as an appropriate framework for the analysis of organizational change. Hence, I proposed the analysis of "what" has changed (content), "how" management changes and communication changes are related (a description of the process, restricted to their consequential relationship), and "why" the change was successful (an explanation of their consequential relationship). Therefore, this case study is explanatory in nature (Yin, 1994: 6). This research is based on a case study strategy, and it must satisfy certain requirements that are specific to the study of this nature, which is confirmed later (see Section 4.5).

4.2   Theoretical framework

4.2.1   Agency, encounters, communication, and organization

Agency is fundamental to the existence of organizations, as it performs organizational reproduction and change. According to ST, agency is the transformative capacity that allows agents to be able "to make a difference" in reality, which cannot be confused with action (the continuous flow of monitored activities), intent (the search for predicted effects), or rationalization (the explanation of action) (Giddens, 1984: 1–16), and agents use resources as a means of transformative capacity (Giddens, 1979: 92, 93; 1984: 258–262). Thus, applying agency refers to transforming reality, and being an agent means being endowed with transformative capacity. However, this perspective of resources as a potential means of agency reduces the agentic capacity of technology to change organizational communication, as emphasized by CT and ANT.

According to ANT, agency can be the resource or result of action (Latour, 1994: 33); to be an actant means being able to affect another actant's course of action (Latour, 2005a), and therefore, "to do, is to make happen" (Latour, 1996: 237). Actants are transformed into actors when they acquire a figuration, a theory of action that mediates and explains their agency (Latour, 2005a: 71, 57, 58), and actors arise as a result of a battle or a negotiation (Callon and Latour, 1981: 279). Thus, to be an actant is to be a carrier of change. However, this perspective does not distinguish actants according to their organizational nature, which makes it difficult to analyze the diversity of agentic capacity at different organizational levels.

According to CT, agency means "to make a difference," can be performed by entities with different ontologies (Cooren, 2006: 82), and can be individual or collective (Taylor and Van Every, 2011: 62). Agency is co-oriented and allows continuous communication (Taylor, 2006: 147), as well as establishes relationships between agents around objects toward which they are mutually oriented (Taylor and Van Every, 2000: 89), and co-orientation is a dynamic process of conversation that allows the construction of texts by negotiating meanings (Cooren, 2006: 13). Texts have agentic power (Cooren, 2004; Katambwe and Taylor, 2006: 55, 56; Taylor and Van Every, 2011: 94, 95) and constitute the cement of organization (Taylor and Van Every, 2011: 118, 119), the basis of communication (Taylor et al., 2001: 74). Thus, the condition of being an agent is being endowed with transformative capacity, and the condition of being a human agent is being endowed with relational and transformative capacities. However, this perspective tends to restrict the agency of nonhuman entities to texts, which weakens the explanation of the agentic capacity of nontextual entities.

Agency is actualized in encounters. According to ST, social structure is constructed in daily communicational encounters (Giddens, 1979: 97–99; 1984: 31–34) and even casual social encounters constitute elements of social structures (1979: 88). According to ANT, face-to-face encounters between intentional and purposive agents are the site of social science (Latour, 2005a: 192), but there is nothing especially local or human in such intersubjective encounters (Latour, 2005b: 18), which means they are not only locals nor just human. According to CT, interaction through language occurs in informal or formal encounters (Taylor and Van Every, 2000: 35, 36) and encounters produce unpredictable conversations between the actors and trigger unexpected communicational events (Güney, 2006: 28), which means that encounters allow for communicational uncertainty. Thus, encounters are fundamental to communication processes and organizational change. These theories recognize the importance of encounters to communication, but they seem to be excessively optimistic regarding the actants' freedom to construct the encounters in which they are involved. In fact, these theories devalue management models and organizational forms. These considerations lead to the formulation of the following hypotheses:

H1: The management models affect encounters and communicational agency.
H2: The management models affect the ontological diversity of the actants involved, which changes communication.

Communication is a constituent of an organization. According to ST, signification is a dimension of social structures (Giddens, 1979: 39, 82; Giddens, 1984: 73) and is structured through language (Giddens, 1979: 106, 107), which is the basis of communication (Giddens, 1984: 264). Interpretative schemas are the modality of signification, and these schemas are standardized elements of the stock of knowledge that are applied by actors in their interactions (Giddens, 1979: 83). The literature has understood the concept of interpretative schemes in different ways: representations of the structures of signification or organizational rules (Orlikowski, 1992: 404), categories and assumptions (Orlikowski, 2000), results of the interaction between old and new understandings (Bartunek, 1984), values and interests (Ranson et al., 1980), social cognitive schemata (Leblebici et al., 1983: 166), and cognitive constructions (Suchan, 2001: 136). For the purposes of this study, I regard interpretative schemas as organizational concepts that are cognitive and normative, theoretical and practical, the use of which permits the production and sharing of meanings and evaluations of organizational situations and transformations. These theoretical assumptions lead to the formulation of the following hypothesis:

H3: Changes in interpretative schemas alter human actants' capacity for meaning.

According to ANT, communication is the association of motion between different ontologically compatible and networked entities. Society and technology are ontologically compatible (Latour, 1994), and the breaking of ontological barriers allows the admittance of a greater diversity of actants in the network (Lee and Stenner, 1999: 110). Society is not a domain but a movement of reassociation or reassembly that is operated by translations (Latour, 2005a: 7–9), sets of relationships between different projects, objectives, or objects (Latour, 1987), which are connections that convey transformation and may generate traceable associations (Latour, 2005a: 108). Network communication involves intermediaries, which are entities that convey messages without transforming them, and mediators, which are entities that transform, translate, distort, and modify the messages they convey (Latour, 2005a: 39). Thus, ANT emphasizes the participation of different actants in communication processes that take place along networks through mediations and intermediations. However, as the attribution of meaning is an integral element of social practices (Giddens, 1979: 39) and message reception is always an act of codification (Thayer, 1968: 27), intermediation is restrictive to nonhuman actants. These theoretical assumptions lead to the formulation of the following hypothesis:

> *H4:* Increasing the number of nonhuman actants improves both the certainty of a communication process and the conformity of human practices.

According to CT, communication is the relationship between different ontologically compatible entities that is oriented toward sharing and solving practical problems. The organization is functional and pragmatically communicational, and communication is always organizational (Taylor and Cooren, 1997: 435, 436); communication is the very condition for an organization's existence, as it circumscribes and instates the organization (Taylor, 1993: 112, 113) and organizes and creates order (Cooren, 2000) through the processes of transforming texts into conversations (Cooren, 2001; Taylor et al., 1996) and conversations into texts (Taylor and Van Every, 2000: 210, 211). The term "emergent organization" refers to an organization that is based on an ongoing social process of interpretation (Taylor et al., 2001) through the daily sensemaking produced by its members (Weick, 1995), as the organization only exists in discourse (Taylor and Cooren, 1997: 428, 429) and emerges in communication (Taylor and Van Every, 2000: 4). Organizations generate texts, verbal or nonverbal, written or nonwritten (Taylor, 1993: 219), and actants may have a different ontological nature, textual or nontextual (Cooren et al., 2011: 1152). However, despite this epistemological enlargement for texts and this ontological opening for actants, CT tends to focus solely on textual communication performed by textual actants, which implies the overvaluation of the agentic capacity of texts and the devaluation of the agentic capacity of nonhuman and nontextual actants. These theoretical considerations lead to the formulation of the following hypothesis:

> *H5:* The creation of new texts supports and animates change in a system of organizational processes.

4.3   Authority, responsibility, empowerment, and communication

These theories associate authority with communication, but they do not sufficiently recognize its value as a constituent of organizations. According to ST, the uses of authority mark the types of control (Giddens, 1984: 157); authoritative resources permit the organization of social time–space, the production/reproduction of the body, the organization of life chances (Giddens, 1984: 258–262), and the creation of frames of meaning as mediators of practical activity (Giddens, 1976: 113); authorization allows the use of allocative resources to achieve command over persons (Giddens, 1979: 100). Thus, authority is linked to domination and signification; however, the relationship between authority and authorization is not sufficiently analyzed, and its rules and formal nature are not properly valued. According to ANT, authority is associated with the authority argument, common sense, and formal position management (Latour, 1987: 31, 192, 232), which is regarded as a social immanence (Law and Hassard, 1999: 65), as well as a basis for communication (Latour, 2005: 155) and for governance (Latour, 1993: 20, 27). Thus, authority is associated with arguments, positions, and social processes, but its importance is neither conceptualized nor recognized in the constituent processes of networking. According to CT, authority allows an organization to legitimate texts, and its legitimizing capacity depends on the positions (Taylor, 1993: 219) that are distributed and made possible by the texts (Taylor and Van Every, 2000: 63, 242). Thus, authority is associated with textualization, but textual (re)production is not the only form of the materialization of authority. Beyond speeches, authority may be associated with noncommunicational factors that are also relevant to organizational management, concretely, rational-legal, traditional, charismatic (Weber, 1964: 358–363), and professional competence (Etzioni, 1964; Mintzberg, 1979: 348–379). None of the theories described earlier adopts an adequate conceptualization of authority, the omission of which might be a way to avoid the existence of agentic constraints.

These theories address power as a fundamental concept, but they devalue the concept of empowerment. According to ST, power means transformative capacity embodied in a series of events that influence their course through resources (Giddens, 1979: 256; Giddens, 1984: 14–16). According to ANT, power is the final result of a process (Latour, 2005: 63, 64) that sustains networks as assemblages of forces (Brown and Capdevila, 2005: 38, 39). CT permits the adoption of the definitions of power provided by ST and ANT (Taylor and Van Every, 2000: 151, 152, 164, 165). Although the concept of empowerment may not be used by these theories, they tacitly admit the importance of empowerment inasmuch as they recognize that power is a process rather than a resource. However, they devalue the unavoidable organizational importance of authority and responsibility, which are reciprocally linked, and their coupling with empowerment. Hence, considering the theoretical considerations described earlier, the following hypotheses may be formulated to link those theories to authority and encounters:

> *H6:* Rational and professional authority influences the assignment of communication tasks to individuals and/or teams.
>
> *H7:* Authority determines the legitimate power to produce texts that possess the capacity for transformation and circulate in networks.
>
> *H8:* Empowerment affects both the nature and frequency of encounters between operators and their chiefs and between functional teams in a plant.

Responsibility is fundamental to the change and reproduction of structures, and it influences organizational communication. According to ST, responsibility is regarded as the context of moral justification that provides arguments to legitimate action (Giddens, 1993: 79). Being responsible for one's actions involves exposing the reasons that justify them and specifying the normative base that legitimates them (Giddens, 1984: 30), basing one's responses upon accounts/justifications/excuses offered by others (Giddens, 1993: 78). Although this concept connects responsibility and communication, it is very limiting because this connection is restricted to the expressed legitimation of actions and ignores that the connection involves not only meaning but also the functional contents of jobs and the formal and professional authority to execute tasks.

According to ANT, responsibility is conceptualized as being endowed with a small capacity for translation. Responsibility may have a legal and social origin (Latour, 2005a: 231) and is attributable to actors (Latour, 1987: 118–120) that are dispersed in a network composed of co-responsibilities (Law and Hassard, 1999: 92, 93). However, in ANT, actors do not benefit from agentic capacities that justify their responsibility (Waelbers, 2011: 33–41). Thus, the conceptualization of responsibility does not consider the different sources or different levels of authority, nor is it associated with agentic capacity.

According to CT, responsibility is conceptualized as a textualizing factor. Responsibility is regarded as a set of rights and obligations that bind individuals to patterns or associations, which frame discourse and its interpretation (Taylor and Van Every, 2000: 102). The responsibility of agency can be shared and can be attributed to individuals or organizations on behalf of which they act (Cooren, 2006: 87, 88), (re)producing the social structures in interactions (Varey, 2006: 193). Responsibility is associated with charges, as supervisors are responsible for the actions of their subordinates, who act by teleaction (Cooren, 2006: 87, Taylor and Van Every, 2000: 88). Additionally, the empowerment of accounting depends on technology (Taylor and Van Every, 2011: 149), knowledge concerning the relationship between texts and organizational practices, and the personal power of agents (Taylor, 1993: 28; Taylor and Van Every, 2011: 178). Hence, accounting is understood as constitutive of the organization and dependent on agents' power to formulate meanings and senses. This approach to responsibility recognizes its agentic value but does not consider its unique nature, as it does not establish clear relationships with technology requirements and personal competencies.

These theories do not provide an adequate framework for analyzing the relationship among technologies, positions, responsibilities, empowerment, communication processes, and organizational change because they do not address the complexity of the organizational network and, consequently, simplify their practical linkages. However, they have hermeneutical virtue and can inspire the analysis of change. These theoretical considerations induce the formulation of the following hypotheses, which connect the content of those theories and the content of the critiques to their theoretical precepts:

> *H9:* The redefinition of team leaders' competence profiles, operational authority, and responsibility increased the production of legitimate discourses of change.
>
> *H10:* The valuation of formal communication increased the responsibility of the agents involved in the production network.
>
> *H11:* The personal competences for interpersonal communication affect the assignment of individuals to leadership positions.
>
> *H12:* The reinforcement of nonhuman actants in production processes increased the product/process recordings and reinforced the responsibility and responsibilization of human actants.

4.4   *Technologies, resources, and communication*

According to ST, agency is based on resources. Systems technology integrates not only automated devices but also human activities (Giddens, 1979: 74), which are structured. Structures are sets of rules and resources preserved as memory traces and marked by the "absence of the subject" (Giddens, 1984: 25), and agency is the transformation of reality that is marked by the capability of agents to exercise power (Giddens, 1984: 14). Hence, structures depend on memorized sets of resources and rules and on the ongoing agency of individuals. Technical devices are regarded as allocative resources of action that are integrated in control systems and, supposedly, under the control of human agency, which is a theoretical option that is not permitted by the other theories, the perspectives of which accord agency to nonhuman actants.

According to ANT and CT, agency is a hybrid relation, which transforms resources into actants. Agency is the relationship between individuals, that is, ongoing, managed co-orientation made possible by communication processes (Taylor, 2006: 150), "a situationally embedded connection of connections between heterogeneous entities" (Robichaud, 2006: 102). Action is shared among actants, whether they are persons, machines, instruments, documents, signs, or buildings (Latour, 1996), and action is a hybrid because it tends to mobilize "the participation of entities with variable ontologies" (materials and symbolic, human and nonhuman) (Cooren, 2006: 82). In the case studied, organizational changes had been performed by human and nonhuman agencies and embodied in material and symbolic realms.

These theories do not adequately address the technology involved in organizational (re)production. The internal environment of factories is deeply characterized by technologies composed of devices and linkages, prescriptions and procedures, interdictions and permissions, authorities and responsibilities, power and empowerment, and measurement and monitoring, which constitute a constraining environment for nonhuman and human agencies. Considering the characteristics of the internal environment, agency may not be exercised as freely as these theories prescribe. However, the approach to resources they provide leads to the formulation of the following hypothesis, which connects their understanding of resources with the critiques of their theoretical omissions:

> *H13:* The improvement of technologies implies an increase in hybrid relationships, which improves communication performance.

4.5   Research strategy

This research adopts a case study strategy, which requires contextualizing the phenomenon under investigation. The phenomenon should be studied in its context (Halinen and Törnroos, 2005: 1286; Hammersley and Gomm, 2000: 6; Mitchell, 2000: 182, 183), and whatever fieldwork approach is selected, theory should be able to explain the phenomenon in its present context and in other contexts (Calder et al., 1982: 242; McGrath and Brinberg, 1983: 116). The organizational change I analyzed here occurred in a factory that mass-produced car devices based on flexible automation. The factory's productivity and quality standards were unsatisfactory, and it had already been slated for relocation to a country where labor was cheaper. To save the factory, a new production director was appointed, who led a profound, extensive, and wide change process. This research was performed over 2 years.

A case research strategy should adopt an approach that privileges the organization as a system. The analysis should regard the phenomenon as a totality, according to an holistic view, and not as a sum of its parts (Gummesson, 1991: 76), or as a whole (the case is the unit) (Rowley, 2002: 22; Yin, 1994: 42), to facilitate the analysis of the case's complexity (Stake, 2000: 440). Hence, the study of this phenomenon encompasses communicational, organizational, social, and technological dimensions and comprises human and nonhuman transformational agencies.

The research process should respect methodological requirements that are specific to this research strategy—credibility (internal validity) and dependability (reliability). Credibility entails correct and reasonable data, correct interpretations, external and internal logical consistency, and the use of methods appropriate for the problem considered (Gummeson, 1991: 161), that is, congruence between sources and findings (Lincoln and Guba, 1985: 213), which can be improved by presenting the interpretations to respondents and peers (Hirschman, 1986: 244, 245), peers' scrutiny of the research project, and thick description (Shenton, 2004: 64–69). The credibility of findings, which were formulated on the basis of participant observation techniques, is ensured by their comparison with theory and by their evaluation by the factory managers directly involved in the change, who numbered 23 persons. Thus, all findings presented here were discussed and consensually approved by the heads of the production, logistic, development, and engineering departments, who participated in evaluating change process meetings, according to their participation in the change being made and their direct knowledge of changes that were implemented. There were two types of these meetings: interdepartmental, which involved the department heads and were intended to analyze departmental cooperation and shared processes, and intradepartmental, which involved the department heads, section heads, and line/cell heads and were intended to analyze the impact of changes in the processes performed by or involving each department.

Dependability concerns the stability of the data and of the researchers as human research instruments (Guba, 1981: 86; Hirschman, 1986: 245). Thus, it comprises both the rational stability of the data and instrument trackability (Guba, 1981: 81), which can be ensured by overlapping methods (Guba, 1981: 86, 87) and data processing techniques (Lincoln and Guba, 1985: 333–336). This research ensures dependability by triangulating the data sources (discourses of heads of lines/cells, sections and departments, written procedures, production records) and the data-gathering techniques (interview, document analysis, and direct observation).

4.6   Results and discussion

The organizational change examined here affected organizational performance, as demonstrated by objective and subjective facts.

Objective results: the quality index improved substantially and the values were reduced by 1/2 or 3/4; the productivity index exhibited the same tendency to improve, going from 700 devices per line, with 42 persons, to between 1100 and 1300 devices per line, with 25 persons.

Subjective results: there was an increased competition between assembly teams, which is symbolized by, in addition to the brand's prestigious reputation among clients, productivity and quality performance criteria. Two years later, the annual meeting of global factory managers, the leaders of the worldwide factories, was held at this factory to gather examples of best practices and adopt benchmarks, thereby contributing to the universalization of management models, processes, and practices; in recognition of his highly successful management of the change in the production department, the head of that department was promoted to factory director.

The change process was stimulated and achieved by a different and complementary set of improvement measures, comprising diverse organizational areas, which transformed the communication dimension and, through this transformation, affected organizational performance. The change actions and their consequences are grouped as follows.

4.6.1   Application of new management methods to the factory's activities

The results show that change encompasses the implementation of new production methods, which has consequences for communication processes. The following new methods were, totally or partially, implemented at the plant: kanban, six sigma quality, lean production, individual functional flexibility, team multifunctional flexibility, and assembly cells; in different ways, all of these models entailed increased cooperation and an improved information system, which led to the optimization of the production flow.

Enhancement of organizational communication: these production methods implied substantial changes in communication processes, including informal and, above all, formal and foreseen, verbal and nonverbal, intradepartmental and interdepartmental, and internal and external communication processes. The effects on internal communication were more pronounced than those on external communication because the commercial process is centralized in the company's headquarters. All heads of departments acknowledged the implementation of these technological innovations and agreed with the consequences that were identified in the analysis.

The results suggest that the introduction of those managerial methods increased quality and productivity, which is strengthened by the findings of the literature review. Six sigma is a rigorous approach to quality management that is intended to realize error-free processes (Pyzdek and

Keller, 2014: 3); the approach is based on an understanding of quality that is based on providing value for customers and providers in all aspects of a business relationship (Harry et al., 2010: 1–5) and values for internal and external communication (Pyzdek and Keller, 2014: 54–62). Lean production plants critically depend on the human resource factor (MacDuffie, 1995; MacDuffie and Krafcik, 1992: 211, 212), individual functional flexibility, and team multifunctional flexibility (Karlsson and Åhlström, 1995: 82), and they employ more team meetings on problem solving, employee suggestions, quality feedback (Forza, 1996: 59), and the documentation of procedures (Forza, 1996: 59). The kanban method implies the use of cards that provide information on production needs (Deleersnyder et al., 1989; Mitra and Mitrani, 1990). These production methods imply substantial changes in communication processes, both as a desired/intended consequence and as an essential/unavoidable outcome. The heads of departments recognized these methodological changes in production processes and agreed on their consequences.

Given the results and these theoretical statements, we can recognize that (1) ST, ANT, and CT do not capture all aspects of management models because they are a structuration resource, but not an allocative or authoritative resource, they are a virtual type of networking factor rather than a material type of networking factor, and they represent a text frame rather than a text. Additionally, we can conclude that (2) the impact of the implementation of new production methods depends on their effects on information and communication agency and that (3) their success depends on the extent to which they improve hybrid relationships performed by actants that are ontologically different. Based on these findings, H13 (the improvement of technologies implies an increase in hybrid relationships, which improves communication performance) is corroborated.

4.6.2   *Coupling organizational units, organizational levels, and the units' members*

The results reveal that change comprises the reconceptualization of relationships between departments.

Reduction of departmentalization effects: under pressure from the production director, the logistics department moved into the factory, the project department increased the presence of its members in the factory and the directors of departments abandoned scheduled flexibility to ensure that individuals with greater formal authority would be present at the factory and at the same time to facilitate corrective decision making.

Redefinition of the importance of the production department: the plant was defined as the factory's functional center, and consequently, the directors of the indirect departments were invited to locate closer to the production director, who was their main internal client. The heads of departments and nearly all other managers agreed on the impact of this transformation that intensified and improved communication between the directors of departments and their team members, which led to the sharing of production goals and to the coupling of their activities. It must be emphasized that, to the extent this change reduced their operational autonomy, the heads of indirect departments had reasons to oppose this change.

Theory suggests that departmentalization might have negative effects, which were substantially corrected through this reform. Functional departmentalization defines departments by the functions that they perform (DuBrin, 2012: 268) and aggregates the same or similar activities (Griffin, 2012: 162). It also stimulates the differentiation in perceptions of the organization and encourages conflicts between departments (Lawrence and Lorsch, 1985: 90; Selznick, 1957: 15), reduces organizational effectiveness and efficiency (Freeman and Cameron, 1993), and creates barriers to communication and shared meanings. The reconceptualization of the centrality of the plant reduced the undesirable effects of departmentalization that damage communicational agency and organizational sustainability.

Considering the empirical results and theoretical contributions, we can conclude that the organizing concept affects (1) the functional relationships between organizational units and (2) encounters and communication processes and the factory's capacity to couple departmental and individual agencies. Thus, H1 (the management models affect encounters and communicational agency) is corroborated. In addition, this proposition should be reformulated as follows: management models affect encounters and communicational agency, which impacts the links between organizational units.

The functional levels of management were reduced from five to three hierarchical levels—heads of line/cell, heads of section, and heads of department—by the elimination of the levels of team leader and heads of shift. This hierarchical downsizing reduced the number of levels involved in information and decision making, reducing interactions between different levels of management, and fostered communication between organizational levels, improving the prevention of problems and the resolution of unexpected problems. The heads of the production department supported this conclusion regarding this impact on organizational communication, and in addition, they emphasized the importance of retraining the heads of line to improve interpersonal communication (see Section 4.6.5).

The results are in line with the prior literature. According to the argument that improved communication represents an effect of downsizing, downsizing enhances communication and decision making (De Meuse et al., 1997: 168; De Meuse and Dai, 2012: 281). The results and the theoretical statements permit us to conclude that (1) downsizing can be focused on improving the communication process rather than simply optimizing organizational resources and that (2) improved communication may increase the speed and quality of decisions. Thus, the findings allow us to conclude that H1 (management models affect encounters and communicational agency) is further supported.

The number of functional meetings increased, such that every line and cell had to hold 5 min meetings that addressed production problems, the realization of quality and productivity goals and proposals to improve processes, which facilitates the information processes. Similarly, a specialized supply team for the assembly lines and cells was created, and the supplying process was based on the kanban method, which entails successive encounters based on shared production process information. The heads of all production departments supported the increase in the diversity of formal meetings and agreed that interpersonal communication had been improved.

Accordingly, theory emphasizes the importance of the human and nonhuman encounters for organizational (re)production. The cell team members participate in regular encounters to analyze process performance (Edosomwan, 1995: 159) in daily encounters to share production and safety information (Black, 1999: 482). The kanban system extracts and disseminates information through cards (kanban) that allow for coordination between cells (Mitra and Mitrani, 1990: 1548), that is, it disciplines operational performance (Deleersnyder et al., 1989). Considering the empirical results and these theoretical assertions, we can conclude that (1) the organization of cells and the kanban method stimulated or required formal encounters, both scheduled and accidental, and that (2) implementation of change benefits from increasing the number of encounters between human actants and between human and nonhuman actants. This means that H2 (the management models affect the ontological diversity of the actants involved, which changes communication) is corroborated.

4.6.3 Mechanization of production based on computerized and electronic machines

The results show that organizational change enabled the improvement of communication based on the control of production process and human agency.

Reinforcement of quality control: the industrial process received machines equipped with electronic devices that reinforced the quality control of the components implanted on the circuit board; these devices also controlled for short circuits and open circuits and were designed to detect every malfunction; their displays, lights, and sounds informed operators of the existence of product nonconformities and suspended the production process, thereby requiring intervention by the machines' operators; the entire process is then repeated for all nonconforming items, and during the first operation, all previous data are erased and the component will pass through all quality control checkpoints.

Improvement of data recording: it involves control over the history of each part before packaging; the passage of items through quality control checkpoints was now registered using barcodes; all information contained in the barcodes of products that were set aside for repair are deleted, and it is necessary to return them to the beginning of the production process and not, as was the case before the reform, to whatever point on the line the operator who performed the repair decided.

The increase of human agency control: it involves the accumulation of data sets containing historical information that can be used to control and improve practices and to record operator performance over time; the relationship between human actants and nonhuman actants is realized through technical protocols, which include instructions regarding operation modes, maintenance modes, and repair modes. Heads of the production and of the product development and engineering departments agreed that these changes improved the control of production processes based on automatic registration and information, thereby enhancing human and nonhuman agency.

The reviewed literature emphasizes the importance of this technological change for the transformation of production and communication agencies. On one hand, change is facilitated by the adoption of computer systems (Alter, 1980; Groover, 1987), by intelligent software that provides feedback for communication between users and machines and between machines and other machines (Majchrzak, 1988: 17, 18), and by visual control in manufacturing plants, such as displays to indicate breakdowns in production and manual card-based production control systems (Bonvik et al., 1997). Hence, the introduction of devices equipped with computerized and electronic functions creates new forms of agency (Cooren, 2006: 98). On the other hand, models of automation imply that human performance is important in monitoring and intervention (Kaber and Endsley, 2004: 120), enhance continuous monitoring based on computational infrastructures (Groover, 2001: 79–106), and integrate multiple automated, guided vehicles and computers to control material handling, coupled with dedicated wired or wireless communication (Kaighobadi and Venkatesh, 1994: 39). Hence, man–machine communication creates new possibilities for performance monitoring and control (Hon, 1995: 150). Considering the results and the reviewed literature, we can conclude that (1) improving quality control requires increasing the number and agentic capacity of nonhuman actants and that (2) it is possible to improve the human actants' performance by regulating their agency using nonhuman actants. Thus, H4 (increasing the number of nonhuman actants improves both the certainty of a communication process and the conformity of human practices) is corroborated.

4.6.4 Empowerment of heads and members of operational units

The results reveal that change encompasses the social representation of the role of unit heads and enhancing their communication abilities.

Increasing the presence of the heads of section in the plant: the heads of section rarely left their offices, and the team leaders served as errand boys, who transported information to the heads of section. Following the reform, they are all required to be present in the factory, assisting and managing the workers assigned to their lines and cells.

Revaluation of the operational rank of the head of line/cell: as they controlled the production and the product, their formal authority was revised to include ensuring the performance of coworkers and of indirectly related departments. These heads of line/cell are now regarded as more important operational elements in the factory than are the heads of departments.

Valuation of signification and communication capacities: the changed authority of chiefs and the increased empowerment of employees required improved signification ability with respect to verbal and nonverbal signs to identify machine damages, workstation conditions, assembly cells, production instructions, and quality procedures. These changes entail the improvement of chiefs' soft skills, such as interpersonal communication, which is necessary to motivate performance and to achieve higher performance levels.

Valuation of scheduling meetings: foreseen and unforeseen meetings increased, as they allow information, coordination, and control in carrying out tasks. The heads of the production department recognized this set of actions and agreed on their consequences.

These positive impacts on communication processes and operational performances align with the reviewed literature. Empowerment stimulates the improvement of team performance (Kirkman and Rosen, 1999: 69), as teamwork is based on transferring tasks and responsibility to workers and encouraging them to proactively assess and resolve production problems (Thompson and Wallace, 1996). Empowering the teams and their members to fulfill their responsibilities (Cawsey and Deszca, 2007: 409) and their participation in decision-making processes encourages shared understandings of responsibility meanings and personnel implications (Bryant and Kazan, 2013) and improved organizational communication (Chen et al., 1997: 861), which is necessary for cross-functional integration (Kitazawa and Sarkis, 2000: 228). Thus, empowerment increases team members' access to information and achieves greater communication and coordination across teams (Kirkman and Rosen, 1999: 71) and, simultaneously, depends on communication processes (Kanter, 1990: 161, 162; Malone, 1997: 23–25), which improve the organization's confidence in performing proactive, interpersonal, and integrative tasks (Sharon, 1988: 849).

Hence, empowerment consists of reinforcing agentic capacity, and it is, simultaneously, a factor and a product of signification and communication processes.

These theoretical considerations alone are insufficient for analyzing the empowerment observed in this case, which must be complemented by a review of the human resource management literature (see Section 4.6.5). Considering the empirical data and the theoretical traits, it is possible to conclude that (1) empowerment entails the formal attribution or redistribution of responsibilities and (2) empowered agentic performance is influenced by positions' responsibilities and personal capacities. Additionally, it is possible to conclude that (3) realizing empowerment implies a larger number of planned and unplanned meetings and that (4) increasing organizational meetings offers new opportunities for enhancing signification and communication abilities of empowered persons. Based on these findings, we can conclude that H6 (rational and professional authority influence the assignment of communication tasks to individuals and/or teams) and H8 (empowerment affects both the nature and frequency of encounters between operators and their chiefs and between functional teams in a plant) are corroborated.

4.6.5   Human resource management

The results show that change comprises the improvement of the abilities of both teams and persons and performance monitoring.

Improvement of human actants' and teams' abilities: redefine the requirements for employee recruitment and selection; adopt and implement a performance evaluation model; and increase professional training programs related to the new management methods and quality concepts.

Improvement of the criteria for establishing teams: create new teams, composed of younger and more qualified workers who have secondary education, are hired under a temporary work regime, and are more capable of stimulating the discovery of new productivity and quality systems; hire new heads of line who are younger and more qualified, have engineering degrees, and possess the operational and communicational skills to be line/cell leaders to legitimate the new production system and lead the change within the teams.

Improvement of the monitoring of the human actants' performance: continuously measure team performance and increase the availability of results on table boards that will allow for both self-control and control by others; adopt a performance assessment model and a productivity and quality prize to reward the teams' performance; and increase human actants' performance records and reports. The heads of the production department agreed on the importance of these transformations for improving the quality and productivity of the assembly process.

These results are in accord with the reviewed literature. Recruitment and selection affect individual and organizational performance because they have a substantial influence on employees' skills (Huselid, 1995: 637; Keep, 1992: 320). Training and development processes affect individual and organizational productivity (Bartel, 1994: 423, 424) and wages (Hutchens, 1989). Performance evaluation makes it possible to align personal goals with organizational goals (Harris, 1983: 272, 273) and facilitates decision-making regarding compensation, promotion, and worker retention issues (Carrell et al., 2000: 225). Evaluation and reward systems affect the performance of individuals and teams (Huselid, 1995: 637, 638; Libby and Thorne, 2009). Leaders' personal characteristics have a meaningful impact on their followers' reaction to change (Oreg and Berson, 2011: 653), and transformative leaders develop team communication and conflict management skills and promote team cohesion (Dionne et al., 2004: 182). Hence, the organizational change requires the rationalization of the human resource management and the requalification of individuals involved in leading team members.

The results and the theoretical considerations allow us to conclude that (1) improving human actants' abilities supports performance improvement and organizational change, (2) the rationalization of human resource management stimulates the development of new concepts related to quality and productivity performance, (3) the replacement of teams' heads enhanced the production of texts that support the signification and legitimation of change, and (4) the change of meaning that these texts induced became essential for improving the alignment of individual, team, and organizational goals. Hence, H3 (changes in interpretative schemas alter human actants' capacity for meaning), H7 (authority determines the legitimate power to produce texts that possess the capacity for transformation and circulate in networks), H9 (the redefinition of team leaders' competence profiles, operational authority, and responsibility increased the production of legitimate discourses of change), and H11 (the personal competences for interpersonal communication affect the assignment of individuals to leadership positions) are corroborated. Additionally, H5 (the creation of new texts supports and animates changes in an organizational process system) is intuitively corroborated. However, the analysis of this hypothesis is hampered because, although a change requires legitimacy, this reflection is focused on the content of the change and not on the process by which the change was implemented and, therefore, fails to account for the legitimation process.

The results also revealed the positive impacts of bureaucratic procedures on organizational performance. The increased formalization of procedures, system documentation, and data recording related to production, maintenance, supplying, planning, doing, controlling, and acting reinforced the traceability of decisions and enhanced personnel responsibility. The heads of the departments recognized the effects of these actions in improving the controllability of production processes.

The literature review reinforces the importance of bureaucracy in determining organizational performance. Bureaucracy is the most effective mass control system (Weber, 1964: 58), and firms endowed with high levels of formalization, specialization, and administrative intensity can achieve better performance (Sine et al., 2006: 130) because formalization increases job codification and improves job descriptions (Hage and Aiken, 1967: 79), standardizes the contributions of individuals to organizational performance (Lawler III, 1994: 4), and improves procedures and record keeping (Seaver, 2001: 23). The importance of documentation reflects the importance of information systems for quality improvement in advanced manufacturing settings (Suresh and Meredith, 1985) and the impact of textualizing the change as an object that stimulates organizational change (Anderson, 2004: 155, 156). Thus, bureaucratic rationalization transforms formal procedures into agentic guidelines and transforms texts into sources of normative context, and these transformations impact the performance of human actants.

The results and the reviewed literature allow us to conclude that (1) a change in regulation entails data recording; (2) records facilitate the traceability of tasks performed and decisions made, as well as the responsibilization of human actants; and (3) formal textualizing promotes the adoption of the new performance patterns. These findings demonstrate that H10 (the valuation of the formal communication increases the responsibility of the agents involved in the production network) and H12 (the reinforcement of nonhuman actants in production processes increased the product/process recordings and reinforced the responsibility and responsibilization of human actants) are corroborated.

4.6.6   Monitoring and controlling organizational and team performance

The results demonstrate that change encompasses improving quality control of products and processes, which involves the performance of nonhuman and human actants.

Improving quality control of assembly lines: there were no consistently updated data on the productivity and quality of the lines; the heads of the lines possessed the production data, but used them subjectively and unsystematically and did not employ them to monitor production processes; panels were installed on every line that allow the heads of line to register, every hour, data on the parts produced and the percentage of nonconforming components.

Improving product quality control: by replacing human operators or compensating for their operational uncertainty, new machines improved production and quality control, increased the reliability of the detection of nonconformities, and informed human operators of the operations that must be executed to correct production processes.

Improving control of the human actants' movements in the plant: different colored uniforms were assigned to different functional teams to monitor their movements in the plant, which reduced unnecessary and unjustifiable movements. The heads of the production department confirmed these actions and agreed on their effects on the production process.

The results suggest the existence of a relationship among monitoring, information, and performance, which is confirmed by the literature. Monitoring business performance focuses on the comparison between what is foreseen and accomplished and between the plan and results (Lind, 2015: 7), which requires performance measures to monitor past performance and stimulate future actions (Neely et al., 2005: 1256). The analysis, evaluation, and improvement of process performance are based on information systems (Edosomwan, 1995: 196). Quality monitoring leads to corrective actions (Feigenbaum, 1991: 107) and to preventive actions (Crosby, 1979: 82), and it involves continuous assessments of performance with respect to both effectiveness and efficiency (Goetsch and Davis, 2012: 69). Productivity and quality are connected through the goal-setting process, which determines targets, resources, and measures of performance and defines how quality and productivity are jointly managed (Edosomwan, 1995: 66). Thus, the availability of the necessary production data makes quality monitoring possible, which fosters the improvement of quality and productivity performance.

The results indicate that quality control has become more effective and quality performance has been substantially improved, which accords with the reviewed literature. Quality control consists of the confirmation of a product's ability to meet specified requirements (Wealleans, 2005: 17) or to meet standards (Juran and Gryna, 1980: 3), involving the integration of quality development, quality maintenance, and quality improvement (Feigenbaum, 1991: 6), and to pursue problem solving to ensure continuous improvement (Ross and Perry, 1999: 167). Hence, quality control is critical to the continuous improvement of process performance and product compliance, and thus, it may be the most important technology in the production flow.

The results also emphasize the importance of regulating human actants' activity, which is confirmed by the literature on dress codes. The significance of clothing as a device for identification is related to the control context (Joseph, 1986: 75), and the existence of dress codes submits agents to conduct patterns imposed by an external authority (Lurie, 1981: 18). Hence, the meaning of clothes affects agency. It is also a resource for materializing organizational identity based on the consistency of labor values, and it affects the compliance with organizational standards of behavior (Pratt and Rafaeli, 1997: 865–868; Rafaeli and Pratt, 1993: 40–47). Hence, clothing is a set of signs that conveys meanings that communicate identity and facilitate control.

These theoretical considerations and results allow us to conclude that (1) improving quality and productivity levels depends on improving quality control of the performance of nonhuman actants and products and on improving performance control of human actants and (2) the effectiveness of control processes depends on nonhuman actants' agency, which improves data validity and process traceability, the diversity of signs present in the work environment, and the accuracy and updating of performance measures. These findings allow us to conclude that H4 (increasing the number of nonhuman actants improves both the certainty of a communication process and the conformity of human practices) and H13 (the improvement of technologies implies an increase in hybrid relationships, which improves communication performance) are confirmed.

4.7   Conclusions

The organizational change was successful, as the quality and productivity levels were substantially improved, which attracted additional orders from the company's clients. Two years later, the factory was cited as a successful case of organizational change within the industrial group and a benchmark for factory managers worldwide. On the basis of this success, we identified the changes that occurred in the organizational, technological, and social areas, which are articulated and made possible by changes in communication processes. These complementary, consequential, or simultaneous changes created an extraordinary case study: within a multinational industrial group, a factory may be transformed from an example of the worst performance into an example of the best performance within a brief 2-year period.

The changes were inspired by the adoption of a broad perspective of the organization and supported by management models that provided organizational settings, principles, rules, and procedures. The standardized management methods transformed both production and communication systems. Methodological changes in production processes affected communication processes. On the one hand, communication enhances the codes in use and communicational agency. On the other hand, the enhanced communication supports improved quality and productivity. Hence, communication allows and amplifies the impact of management processes on the creation of sustainable outcomes, that is, it ensures the formation of relationships between both structures and agencies and between the macro and micro levels.

Organizational communication is not merely a function of organizational strategy; rather, it is the actual cornerstone of any change strategy. On the one hand, performance depends on the communicational function of machines, which are tendentiously regarded as factors of production rather than factors of communication, despite that their production function may be dependent on their communication function. On the other hand, organizational communication depends on a complex network of signification processes, constituted by either mediation or intermediation, which are, respectively, participated in and updated by human and non-human actants, the agency of which is fundamental to an organization. This complex and wide phenomenon can be examined using the theoretical triangulation of ST, ANT and CT, meaning that these theories provide an adequate framework for organizational change analysis.

References

Alter, S. *Decision Support Systems: Current Practice and Continuing Challenges.* Reading, MA: Addison-Wesley, 1980.

Anderson, D. The textualizing functions of writing for organizational change. *Journal of Business and Technical Communication* 18(2) (2004): 141–164.

Bartel, A. Productivity savings from the implementation of employee training programs. *Industrial Relations* 4 (4) (1994): 411–425.

Bartunek, J. Changing interpretive schemes and organizational restructuring: The example of a religious order. *Administrative Science Quarterly* 29 (1984): 355–372.

Black, J. Design and implementation of lean manufacturing systems and cells. In *Handbook of Cellular Manufacturing Systems*, pp. 453–496. John Wiley & Sons, 1999.

Bonvik, A., Couch, C., and Gershwin, S. A comparison of production-line control mechanisms. *International Journal of Production Research* 35 (3) (1997): 789–804.

Brown, S. and Capdevila, R. Perpetuum mobile: Substance, force, and the sociology of translation. In *Actor Network Theory and After* (3rd edn., pp. 26–50). Malden, MA: Blackwell Publishing, 2005.

Bryant, A. and Kazan, A. *Self-leadership: How to Become a More Successful, Efficient, and Effective Leader from the Inside Out.* New York: McGraw-Hill, 2013.

Calder, B., Phillips, L., and Tybout, A. The concept of external validity. *Journal of Consumer Research* 9 (3) (1982): 240–244.

Callon, M. and Latour, B. Unscrewing the big leviathan: How actors macrostructure reality and how sociologists help them to do so? In *Advances in Social Theory and Methodology: Toward an Integration of Micro and Macro Sociology*, pp. 277–303. London, U.K.: Routledge, 1981.

Carrell, M., Elbert, N., and Hatfield, R. *Human Resources Management: Strategies for Managing a Diverse and Global Workforce*, 6th edn. Fort Worth, TX: The Dryden Press, 2000.

Cawsey, T. and Deszca, G. *Toolkit for Organizational Change.* Thousand Oaks, CA: Sage Publications, 2007.

Chen, A., Sawyers, R., and Williams, P. Reinforcing ethical decision making through corporate culture. *Journal of Business Ethics* 16 (1997): 855–865.

Cooren, F. *The Organizing Property of Communication*. Amsterdam, the Netherlands: John Benjamins Pub. Co., 2000.

Cooren, F. *The Organizing Property of Communication*. New York: John Benjamins Pub. Co., 2001.

Cooren, F. Textual agency: How texts do things in organizational settings. *Organization* 11 (3) (2004): 373–393.

Cooren, F. The organizational world as a plenum of agencies. *Communication as Organizing: Empirical and Theoretical Explorations*. In *The Dynamic of Text and Conversation* (pp. 141–156). Mahwah, NJ: Lawrence Erlbaum Associates, 2006.

Cooren, F., Kuhn, T., Cornelissen, J., and Clark, T. Communication, organizing and organization: An overview and introduction to the special issue. *Organization Studies* 32 (9) (2011): 1149–1170.

Crosby, P. *Quality is Free: The Art of Making Quality Certain*. New York: New American Library, 1979.

De Meuse, K., Bergmann, T., and Vanderheiden, P. Corporate downsizing. separating myth from fact. *Journal of Management Inquiry* 6 (2) (1997): 168–176.

De Meuse, K. and Dai, G. Reducing costs and enhancing efficiency or damaging the company: Downsizing in today's global economy. In *Downsizing: Is Less Still More* (pp. 258–290). Cambridge, U.K.: Cambridge University Press, 2012.

Deleersnyder, J.-L., Hodgson, T., Malek, H., and. O'Grady, P. Kanban controlled pull systems: An analytical approach. *Organization Science* 35 (9) (1989): 1079–1091.

Dionne, S., Yammarino, F., Atwater, L., and Spangler, W. Transformational leadership and team performance. *Journal of Organizational Change Management* 17 (2) (2004): 177–193.

DuBrin, A. *Essentials of Management*, 3rd edn. Mason, OH: South-Western, 2012.

Edosomwan, J. *Integrating Productivity and Quality Management*, 2nd edn. New York: Marcel Dekker, Inc., 1995.

Etzioni, A. *Modern Organizations*. Englewood Cliffs, NJ: Prentice-Hall, 1964.

Feigenbaum, A. *Total Quality Control*, Vol. 1, 3rd edn. New York: McGraw-Hill, 1991.

Forza, C. Work organization in lean production and traditional plants: What are the differences? *International Journal of Operations and Production Management* 16 (2) (1996): 42–62.

Freeman, S. and Cameron, K. Organizational downsizing: A convergence and reorientation framework. *Organization Science* 4 (1) Focused Issue: Organizational decline and adaptation: Theoretical controversies (1993): 10–29.

Giddens, A. *Central Problems in Social Theory: Action, Structure and Contradiction in Social Analysis*. London, U.K.: Macmillan, 1979.

Giddens, A. *New Rules of Sociological Method*, 2nd edn. Stanford, CA: Stanford University Press, 1993.

Giddens, A. *New Rules of Sociological Method*. London, U.K.: Hutchinson, 1976.

Giddens, A. *The Constitution of Society: Outline of Theory of Structuration*, 4th edn. Cambridge, U.K.: Polity Press, 1984.

Goetsch, D. and Davis, S. Strategic management: Planning and execution for competitive advantage. In *Quality Management for Organizational Excellence: Introduction to Total Quality* (7th edn., pp. 67–84). Harlow, U.K.: Pearson, 2012.

Griffin, R. *Fundamentals of Management*, 2nd edn. Mason, OH: South-Western, 2012.

Groover, M. *Automation Production Systems Computer Integrated Manufacturing.* Upper Saddle River, NJ: Prentice-Hall, 2001.

Groover, M. *Automation, Production Systems, and CIM.* Englewood Cliffs, NJ: Prentice-Hall, 1987.

Guba, E. Criteria for assessing the trustworthiness of naturalistic inquiries. *Educational Evaluation and Policy Analysis* 29 (2) (1981): 75–91.

Gummesson, E. *Qualitative Methods in Management Research.* Newbury Park, CA: Sage, 1991.

Güney, S. Making sense of a conflict as the (missing) link between collaborating Actors. In *Communication as Organizing: Empirical and Theoretical Explorations in the Dynamic of Text and Conversation* (pp. 19–36). Mahwah, NJ/London, U.K.: Lawrence Erlbaum Associates Publishers, 2006.

Hage, J. and Aiken, M. Relationship of centralization to other structural properties. *Administrative Science Quarterly* 12 (1) (1967): 72–92.

Halinen, A. and Törnroos, J.-Ä. Using case methods in the study of contemporary business networks. *Journal of Business Research* 58 (2005): 1285–297.

Hammersley, M. and Gomm, R. Introduction. In *Case Study Method* (pp. 2–16). London, U.K.: Sage, 2000.

Harris, O. *Managing People at Work: Concepts and Cases in Interpersonal Behaviour.* Malabar, FL: Robert E. Krieger Publishing Company, 1983.

Harry, M., Mann, P., Hodgins, O., Hubert, R., and Lacke, C. *Practitioner's Guide to Statistic and Lean Six Sigma for Process Improvement.* Hoboken, NJ: John Wiley & Sons, 2010.

Hirschman, E. Humanistic inquiry in marketing research: Philosophy, method, and criteria. *Journal of Marketing Research* 23 (1986): 237–249.

Hon, K.K.B. Performance and evaluation of manufacturing systems. *CIRP Ann—Manufacturing Technology* 54 (2) (1995): 130–154.

Huselid, M. The impact of human resources management practices on turnover, productivity, and corporate financial performance. *Academy of Management Journal* 38 (3) (1995): 635–672.

Hutchens, R. Seniority, wages and productivity: A turbulent decade. *Journal of Economic Perspectives* 3 (4) (1989): 49–64.

Joseph, N. *Uniforms and Nonuniforms: Communication Through Clothing.* New York: Greenwood Press, 1986.

Juran, J. and Gryna, F. *Quality Planning and Analysis*, 2nd edn. New York: McGraw-Hill, 1980.

Kaber, D. and Endsley, M. The effects of level of automation and adaptive automation on human performance, situation awareness and workload in a dynamic control task. *Theoretical Issues in Ergonomics Science* 5 (2) (2004): 113–153.

Kaighobadi, M. and Venkatesh, K. Flexible manufacturing systems: An overview. *International Journal of Operational Production Management* 14 (4) (1994): 26–49.

Kanter, R. *The Change Masters: Corporate Entrepreneurs at Work*, 6th edn. London, U.K.: Unwin Hyman, 1990.

Karlsson, C. and Åhlström, P. Change processes towards lean production: The role of the remuneration system. *International Journal of Operations and Production Management* 15 (11) (1995): 80–99.

Katambwe, J. and Taylor, J. Modes of organizational integration. In *Communication as Organizing: Empirical and Theoretical Explorations in the Dynamic of Text and Conversation* (pp. 55–80). Mahwah, NJ: Lawrence Erlbaum Associates, 2006.

Keep, E. Corporate training strategies: The vital component? In *Human Resource Strategies* (pp. 320–336). London, U.K.: Sage, 1992.

Kirkman, B. and Rosen, B. Beyond self-management: Antecedents and consequences of team empowerment. *Academy of Management Journal* 42 (1) (1999): 58–74.

Kitazawa, S. and Sarkis, J. The relationship between ISO 14001 and continuous source reduction programs. *International Journal of Operational Production Management* 20 (2) (2000): 225–248.

Latour, B. On interobjectivity. *Mind, Culture and Activity* 3 (1996): 228–245.

Latour, B. On recalling ANT. In *Actor Network Theory* (3rd edn., pp. 15–25). Oxford, U.K.: Blackwell, 2005b.

Latour, B. On technical mediation: Philosophy, sociology, genealogy. *Common knowledge* 3 (2) (1994): 29–64.

Latour, B. *Reassembling the Social: An Introduction to Actor-Network Theory.* Oxford, U.K.: University Press, 2005a.

Latour, B. *Science in Action.* Cambridge, MA: Harvard University Press, 1987.

Latour, B. *We Have Never Been Modern.* Cambridge, MA: Harvard University Press, 1993.

Law, J. *Organizing Modernity.* Oxford, U.K.: Blackwell Publishers, 1994.

Law, J. and Hassard, J. (eds.) *Actor Network Theory and After.* Oxford, U.K.: Blackwell, 1999.

Lawrence, P. and Lorsch, J. High-performing organizations in three environments. In *Organization Theory* (pp. 87–105). London, U.K.: Penguin Books, 1985.

Leblebici, H., Marlow, E., and Rowland, K. Research note: A longitudinal study of the stability of interpretative schemas, organizational structure, and their contextual correlates. *Organization Studies* 4 (1983): 2165–2184.

Lee, N. and Stenner, P. Who pays? Can we pay them back? In *Actor Network Theory and After* (pp. 90–112). Oxford, U.K.: Blackwell, 1999.

Libby, T. and Thorne, L. The influence of incentive structure on group performance in assembly lines and teams. *Behavioral Research in Accounting* 21 (2) (2009): 57–72.

Lincoln, Y. and Guba, E. *Naturalistic Inquiry.* Newbury Park, CA: Sage, 1985.

Lind, P. *Monitoring Business Performance: Models, Methods and Tools.* New York: Routledge, 2015.

Lurie, A. *The Language of Clothes.* New York: Random House, 1981.

Macduffie, J. Human resource bundles and manufacturing performance: Organizational logic and flexible production systems in the world auto industry. *Industrial and Labor Relations Review* 48 (2) (1995): 197–221.

MacDuffie, J. and Krafcik, J. Integrating technology and human resources for high-performance manufacturing: Evidence from the international auto industry. In *Transforming Organizations* (pp. 209–226). New York: Oxford University Press, 1992.

Majchrzak, A. *The Human Side of Factory Automation.* San Francisco, CA: Jossey-Bass, 1988.

Malone, T. Is empowerment just a fad? Control, decision making, and IT. *MIT Sloan Management Review* 38 (1997): 23–29.

McGrath, J. and Brinberg, D. External validity and the research process: A comment on the Calder/Lynch dialogue. *Journal of Consumer Research* 10 (1) (1983): 115–124.

Mintzberg, H. *The Structuring of Organizations*. Englewood Cliffs, NJ: Prentice Hall, 1979.

Mitchell, J.C. Case and situation analysis. In *Case Study Method* (pp. 165–186). London, U.K.: Sage, 2000.

Mitra, D. and Mitrani, I. Analysis of a kanban discipline for cell coordination in production lines. *Management Science* 36 (12) (1990): 1548–1566.

Neely, A., Gregory,M., and Platts, K. Performance measurement system design: A literature review and research agenda. *International Journal of Operations and Production Management* 25 (12) (2005): 1228–1263.

Oreg, S. and Berson, Y. Leadership and employees' reactions to change: The role of leaders' personal attributes and transformational leadership style. *Personnel Psychology* 64 (2011): 627–659.

Orlikowski, W. The duality of technology: Rethinking the concept of technology in organizations. *Organization Science* 3 (3) (1992): 398–427.

Orlikowski, W. Using technology and constituting structures: A practice lens for studying technology in organizations. *Organization Science* 11 (4) (2000): 404–428.

Parker, S. Enhancing role breadth self-efficacy: The roles of job enrichment and other organizational interventions. *Journal of Applied Psychology* 83 (6) (1988): 835–852.

Pratt, M. and Rafaeli, A. Organizational dress as a symbol of multilayered social identities. *Academy of Management Review* 40 (4) (1997): 862–898.

Pyzdek, T. and Keller, P. *The Six Sigma*. New York: McGraw-Hill Education, 2014.

Rafaeli, A. and Pratt, M. Tailored meanings: On the meaning and impact of organizational dress. *Academy of Management Review* 18 (1) (1993): 32–55.

Ranson, S., Hinings, B., and Greenwood, R. The structuring of organizational structures. *Administrative Science Quarterly* 25 (1980): 1–17.

Robichaud, D. Steps toward a relational view of agency. In *Communication as Organizing: Empirical and Theoretical Explorations in the Dynamic of Text and Conversation* (pp. 101–114). Mahwah, NJ: Lawrence Erlbaum Associates, 2006.

Ross, J. and Perry, S. *Total Quality Management: Text, Cases and Readings*, 3rd edn. Boca Raton, FL: CRC Press, 1999.

Rowley, J. Using case studies in research. *Management Research News* 25 (1) (2002): 16–27.

Seaver, M. *Implementing ISO 9000:2000*. Burlington, VT: Gower, 2001.

Selznick, P. *Leadership in Administration: A Sociological Interpretation*. New York: Harper and Row, 1957.

Shenton, A. Strategies for ensuring trustworthiness in qualitative research projects. *Education for Information* 22 (2004): 63–75.

Sine, W., Mitsuhashi, H., and Kirsch, D. Revisiting burns and stalker: Formal structure and new venture performance in merging economic sectors. *Academy of Management Journal* 49 (1) (2006): 121–132.

Stake, R. Case studies. In *Handbook of Qualitative Research* (pp. 435–454). Thousand Oaks, CA: Sage, 2000.

Suchan, J. The effect of interpretive schemes on video teleducation's conception, implementation, and use. *Journal of Business and Technical Communication* 15 (2001): 2.

Suresh, N. and Meredith, J. Quality assurance information systems for factory automation. *International Journal of Production Research* 23 (3) (1985): 479–488.

Taylor, J. Coorientation: A conceptual framework. In *Communication as Organizing: Empirical and Theoretical Explorations in the Dynamic of Text and Conversation* (pp. 141–156). Mahwah, NJ: Lawrence Erlbaum Associates Publishers, 2006.

Taylor, J. *Rethinking the Theory of Organizational Communication: How to Read an Organization.* Norwood, NJ: Alex Publishing Corporation, 1993.

Taylor, J. and Cooren, F. What makes communication 'organizational'? How the many voices of a collectivity become the one voice of an organization. *Journal of Pragmatics* 27 (1997): 409–438.

Taylor, J., Cooren, F., Giroux, N., and Robichaud, D. The communicational basis of organization: Between the conversation and the text. *Communication. Theory* 6 (1996): 1–39.

Taylor, J., Flanagin, A., Cheney, G., and Seibold, D. Organizational communication research: key moments, central concerns, and future challenges. In *Communication Yearbook* (pp. 99–138). London, U.K.: Sage, 2001.

Taylor, J. and Van Every, E. *The Emergent Organization: Communication as its Site and Surface.* Mahwah, NJ: Lawrence Erlbaum Associates, 2000.

Taylor, J. and Van Every E. *The Situated Organization: Case Studies in the Pragmatics of Communication Research.* New York: Routledge, 2011.

Thayer, L. *Communication and Communication Systems.* Homewood, IL: Irwin, 1968.

Thompson, P. and Wallace, T. Redesigning production through teamworking: Case studies from the Volvo Truck Corporation. *International Journal Operations and Production Management* 16 (2) (1996): 103–118.

Varey, R. Accounts in interactions: Implications of accounting practices for managing. In *Communication as Organizing: Empirical and Theoretical Explorations in the Dynamic of Text and Conversation* (pp. 181–196). Mahwah, NJ: Lawrence Erlbaum Associates, 2006.

Waelbers, K. *Doing Good with Technologies: Taking Responsibility for the Social Role of Emerging Technologies* (Philosophy of Engineering and Technology). London, U.K.: Spring, 2011.

Wealleans, D. *The Quality Audit for ISO 9001:2000: A Practical Guide*, 2nd edn. Burlington, VT: Gower, 2005.

Weber, M. *The Theory of Social and Economic Organization*, 2nd edn. New York: The Free Press, 1964.

Weick, K. *Sensemaking in Organizations: Foundations for Organizational Science.* London, U.K.: Sage, 1995.

Yin, R. *Case Study Research: Design and Methods*, 2nd edn. Thousand Oaks, CA: Sage, 1994.

chapter five

Electronic human resource management in SMEs

An exploratory study in a Portuguese municipality

Sara Carvalho and Carolina Machado

Contents

Abstract

The advent of technology has revolutionized, among other aspects of our daily life, the business world and, in particular, human resource management (HRM). In recent years, several HRM processes, from recruitment and selection to training or performance appraisal, among others, are increasingly being supported by web-based technology. Electronic-HRM (e-HRM) seems to have a positive impact on HR processes' effectiveness and efficiency, but further and better studies need to be done in order to more definitively confirm this relationship. Although the latest decades have been productive on research on e-HRM, few authors have specifically studied this reality in the context of small and medium enterprises (SMEs). In this work, we present the results of a small exploratory study on e-HRM among a few local SMEs, which have revealed that, in general terms, e-HRM in SMEs is more common among administrative, communication, and recruitment processes.

Keywords: HRM, e-HRM, SME, New technologies, Portugal

5.1   Introduction

> New technologies are all around us. From smart appliances to the Internet, the way we work and live has been profoundly altered by technology—in less than a generation. This is just as true in the field of human resource management....
>
> **Huselid (2004, p. 119)**

The earlier reference contextualizes in a succinct way the main aim of this chapter. Indeed, nowadays we are living in a deeply technological society, where the diversity of tasks, formerly unthinkable, is today possible and where, in many tasks, the human being is helped, or even replaced, by computers. This reality is observed in different areas of our life, diverse activity sectors, and diverse organizational departments—the human resource department is not, indeed, an exception. The generalization of the computer and the Internet use in organizations also allows the introduction of changes in the way some human resource management (HRM) activities are developed.

The main aim of this chapter is to develop a critical literature revision about the use of new technologies in HRM services, with a particular emphasis on small and medium enterprises (SMEs), where the amount of information available is smaller. Also for this reason, the option of complementing the literature revision with the results of a small exploratory study, conducted in the business field of a Portuguese municipality, was made.

5.2   Evolution of technology use in human resource management

Technological changes that took place in the last decades, with the advent of the computer and Internet, have had a considerable impact on the labor world. Indeed, they have contributed not only to process automation, but also to the appearance of new ways of work organization (e.g., telework). These changes forced organizations to adapt to a new reality. Particularly in what concerns HRM, they lead to changes in how to develop, among others, the recruitment, selection, training, and performance appraisal processes.

Until the 1960s, HRM processes were developed manually, but with the advent of new information and communication technologies, automated systems started arising, making it easier to perform HRM administrative tasks (e.g., workers' data record, wage processing) (DeSanctis, 1986; Stone & Dulebohn, 2013).

Later, in the 1980s, these automated systems evolved into software solutions that allowed HR departments to realize different tasks, namely, training, performance appraisal, information record/control about candidates to job offers, and reports development to top management, among others. These new systems were first named human resource information systems (HRIS) (Stone & Dulebohn, 2013). They are "information systems used to acquire, store, manipulate, analyze, retrieve, and distribute pertinent information regarding an organization's human resources" (Kavanagh, Gueutal, & Tannenbaum, 1990, quoted by Stone & Dulebohn, 2013). They are also systems directed, exclusively, to HR professionals (Marler & Fisher, 2013; Ruel, Bondarouk, & Looise, 2004; Strohmeier, 2007).

It was at the end of the 1980s and the beginning of the 1990s that access (to consult and edit) to these databases by HR professionals, as well as by other organization members (e.g., top management, line managers, workers in general), from their workplace, was made possible by HR database installation in central servers attached to the local area network (LAN) or wide area network (WAN), with the appearance of the Internet (Stone & Dulebohn, 2013).

Later, with the appearance of the Internet, this database access became possible anywhere, even outside the organization. Moreover, organizations began to use the Internet to interact with their external stakeholders, for example, through online recruitment systems that allow people from any city in the world to apply to these organizations' job offers. Since then, the designation "electronic human resource management (e-HRM)" has been used to refer specifically to HR electronic systems that focus not only on HR professionals (as with HRIS) but all internal and external stakeholders (Lengnick-Hall & Mortiz, 2003; Marler & Fisher, 2013; Rüel et al., 2004; Stone & Dulebohn, 2013; Strohmeier, 2007).

Authors are not in agreement about the terms used to refer to these concepts. So it is not only possible to find in the literature a great diversity of concepts that are nevertheless related and do not have the same significance (e.g., HRIS, e-HRM, virtual HRM, web-based HRM, intranet-based HRM), but sometimes different authors use the same term to designate different concepts (e.g., they use the expression HRIS to designate what was defined as e-HRM). Here, we have decided to consider Strohmeier's (2007) definition of "e-HRM," as it is one of the most consensual in the literature.

According to Strohmeier, e-HRM systems are a way of "(planning and implementation) application of information technology for both networking and supporting at least two individual or collective actors in their shared performing of HR activities" (p. 20). This definition brings together some e-HRM-relevant aspects. First, it points out the possibility of using information technologies to make networking in HRM easy, allowing the interaction among organizational actors, regardless of the geographical distance between them. On the other hand, it also refers to these technologies as a potential support tool for the development of diverse HRM tasks, replacing (e.g., freeing) partially or totally HR departments in their performance. Furthermore, it still recognizes that e-HRM is a multilevel phenomenon that involves individuals, groups, organizational units, and the organization as a whole that interact with each other, in order to ensure HR activity development (Strohmeier, 2007).

Nowadays, e-HRM systems are used by many organizations in different HR management processes, namely, recruitment, selection, training, compensation, performance management, and HR planning (Eckhardt, Laumer, Maier, & Weitzel, 2014; Stone & Dulebohn, 2013). In 2009, approximately two-thirds of European organizations reported the use of e-HRM systems (Strohmeier & Kabst, 2009). In the United Kingdom, in 2005, the percentage of organizations that used some form of e-HRM was 77% (CIPD, 2005, quoted by Parry & Tyson, 2011).

This raise in this type of system use has also been followed by an increase in this scientific production area. Indeed, the first e-HRM studies had their beginning near 1995. However, the last decade has been fruitful in what concerns this subject. Although most of the studies have been conducted in the United States and Europe, the researchers' focus has been very heterogeneous, covering different kinds of technologies (e.g., HR portals, intranet, software), diverse HRM areas (e.g., e-recruitment, e-learning, e-compensation), different kinds of e-HRM consequences (e.g., costs, efficacy, workers' confidence degree), and at different levels (e.g., micro, meso, and macro) (Strohmeier, 2007). Nevertheless, due to some of these studies' limitations (e.g., a few longitudinal studies; many studies limited to contexts, systems, and specific consequences, not allowing a holistic view of the subject; inconsistent results and, sometimes, contradictory), there still are many e-HRM basic dimensions that need to be understood (Marler & Fisher, 2013; Strohmeier, 2012).

5.3   e-HRM areas

As said earlier, e-HRM has been suffering a very significant evolution in the last decades, spreading to more and more HRM areas or processes, making it possible to find in the literature references to technology use, particularly web-based technology, in different areas such as wage processing, HR planning, recruitment and selection, benefits and compensation, politics, internal communication, training and development, or performance appraisal. However, and it is understandable, in some of these processes, e-HRM is more common than in others, and the interest from the researchers is also different.

As expected, more common applications of information systems to HRM are mainly related to more administrative tasks such as salary processing and employees' database management (Lee, 2007; Ngai & Wat, 2006; Rüel et al., 2004; Strohmeier, 2009). Today, there are few (or none) organizations that manually work on their salary processing, without the more or less complex information system's help. On the other hand, the use of platforms that are available on the Internet (called in the literature as "self-service technologies" or "HR portals") is common, which involves employees in HR planning tasks, making it easy to access and update their information (previously available only on "paper" in HR departments) and increasing, on its side, data correctness, leading to time and cost reduction on the HRM side (Chakrabortya & Mansor, 2013).

Supporting other HR processes, communication (internal and external) is also one of the areas where e-HRM is disseminated, with the very common use of e-mails, intranet, and blogs/forums in any context, facilitating communication among the different organizational actors (Panayotopoulou, Vakola, & Galanaki, 2007).

Beyond administrative tasks and communication, e-recruitment, a recruitment process that appeals to the Internet, e-mail, and corporate websites or job portals (Galanaki, 2002), is undoubtedly the most disseminated e-HRM application area (Eckhardt et al., 2014). With trivialization of the Internet use, in a professional context, more and more organizations spread online job offers (e.g., in their corporate website, job portals, social networks), make online platforms for job application submissions available, or receive curricula vitae by e-mail. On the other hand, there are also more and more candidates that appeal to these same platforms through job posting research and application.

According to Furtmueller, Wilderom, and Tate (2011), in 2011, 40,000 job platforms were permanently available online, and all of the Top 100 international organizations, according to Fortune, recruit online. In Portugal, according to the National Institute of Statistics (INE), in 2013, 24.5% of organizations with more than 10 employees make recruitment offers and forms available at their corporate website. On the other hand, about 23.2% of Portuguese between 16 and 74 years old use the Internet in the first 3 months of the year in order to find a job, respond to job announcements, or send spontaneous applications (INE, 2014). Although the risk of overload of HR departments with curricula vitae is clear, e-recruitment has advantages in terms of time, costs, and candidate diversity that allow to attract potential employees (Ensher, Nielson, & Grant-Vallone, 2002; Nesbeitt, 1999).

Directly related to e-recruitment, although less studied and used, e-selection (the use of web tools to select candidates, namely, curriculum vitae selection made by informatics programs through research by key-words, tests and online application, and videoconferences, among others) has aroused interest in some researchers, as it also reduces the costs and the time spent in HR selection and at the same time facilitates this pro-cess in situations where long distances separate the candidate from the organization (Panayotopoulou et al., 2007). Furthermore, many organi-zations believe that e-selection might be greatly utilized in the future (Chapman & Webster, 2003).

Another area where e-HRM is prevalent is "training." E-mail and the Internet can be easily used to identify training needs, reduce costs (e.g., with paper) and time and also raise the response rate (McClelland, 1994). The only inconvenience is the possible doubts from the inquirer about the preservation of their anonymity (Panayotopoulou et al., 2007).

On the other hand, the Internet and the intranet have also transformed e-learning (electronic learning) as an interesting alternative or comple-ment to face-to-face training. Just do a quick search in a search engine to find dozens of course offers or workshops via e-learning; besides, e-learning platforms are also, nowadays, very common in the academic environment. In 2003, the American Society to Training and Development (presently Talent Management Association) presented the results of a sur-vey according to which 95% of respondents reported using some form of e-learning in their organizations (Ellis, 2003, quoted by DeRouin, Fritzsche, & Salas, 2005).

Despite the lack of consensus about e-learning definition, we can consider it as "the process by which the student learns through contents placed in the computer and/or Internet and where a professor, if exist-ing, is at a distance using the Internet as a way to communicate (syn-chronously or asynchronously) being able to develop intermediate face to face sessions" (Leal & Amaral, 2006, p. 4). By allowing access to train-ing to employees anywhere in the world and reducing costs associated with face-to-face training, e-learning has become a very common practice (Salas, DeRouin, & Littrell, 2005, quoted by Stone & Dulebohn, 2013).

Finally, two other areas of e-HRM application, clearly less studied and about which we have less information, are compensation and benefits management (named by some authors as "e-compensation") and perfor-mance appraisal.

Regarding the first one, it is known that some organizations allow their employees (through the so-called self-service platforms) to define their preferences in terms of compensation and benefits, thereby freeing, in some way, HR professionals. On the other hand, top management can also (through the same type of platforms, this time, called "manager self-service") consult information about their employees' salaries and benefits and make decisions in this respect (e.g., confirm or authorize actions at this level) (Panayotopoulou et al., 2007).

With regard to performance appraisal, e-HRM has allowed, in some organizations, all processes to be conducted online, taking into account that the appraised and the appraiser fulfill directly in the platforms their auto and hetero appraisal forms, respectively. Besides, these platforms allow employees to control their performance and the management to consult information about how to conduct a performance appraisal process or which criterion and measures to consider with each function or job as well as to consult examples and models of effective appraisals (Adamson & Zampetti, 2001, quoted by Panayotopoulou et al., 2007). Moreover, this practice allows the HR department to reduce time and costs (Panayotopoulou et al., 2007).

5.4   e-HRM aims and impact

According to the literature, organizations invest in e-HRM based on three aims: increase efficiency, increase effectiveness, and transform the HRM function, freeing it from administrative tasks and making it a business strategic partner (Bondarouk, Rüel, & van der Heijden, 2009; Lepak & Snell, 1998; Marler, 2009; Ruël et al., 2004). To these three aims, Ruel et al. (2004) add a fourth, which seems to motivate, particularly, large international organizations: improve the organization's global orientation through HR policies and practice standardization and harmonization. Nevertheless, some authors also suggest that organizations do not always clearly define their aims to implement e-HRM; in a majority of situations, its efforts are directed essentially toward efficiency increase and cost reduction (Bondarouk & Ruël, 2013; Parry & Tyson, 2011; Ruël et al., 2004).

The challenge is to understand what the real e-HRM results or consequences are in organizations. Although the investment initially needs to be done in e-HRM systems (in financial terms and time for people to adapt to them), did they become compensatory in the short and medium term? Will it be possible to verify effective cost reduction? Will HR processes be superior in quality? Will the HR manager get a more strategic function, or instead, being replaced by machines, will his job cease to exist? Many authors have been looking to answer these and other questions about e-HRM impact using different methodologies, levels of analysis, and operationalization concepts.

In what concerns e-HRM impact at the efficiency level, although the studies that have been carried out do point to positive results, they are not always conclusive. So some studies have been suggesting an efficiency increase resultant from other diverse e-HRM intermediate consequences, which are also interrelated, such as HRM people reduction, direct cost reduction or the higher speed of processes resulting from its automation, and the involvement of other organizational actors in its implementation (Dery, Grant & Wiblen, 2009; Parry & Tyson, 2011; Rüel et al., 2004; Ruta, 2005; Strohmeier, 2007).

We cannot ignore that some of these advantages result from HRM responsibility changes for line managers and top management (Strohmeier, 2007), the reason why it will be necessary to evaluate if the additional time spent by these organizational actors in the performance of these tasks compensates for the time reduction for HR managers.

The results of these studies should, therefore, be interpreted with some caution, considering that in some of them, the e-HRM impact was evaluated based on the perceptions of the inquired organizational actors (e.g., top management) and not on data and real number consultation and analysis (Parry & Tyson, 2011; Rüel et al., 2004). Although this perception can be seen as an extremely relevant indicator so that organizations, in general, understand the importance in evolving to an e-HRM, it is critical that this kind of data be complemented in the future with more concrete and palpable results.

Another relevant question is related to the additional time that HR managers may need to adapt to e-HRM. Indeed, if, on one hand, these professionals spend less time with administrative and routine tasks, on the other hand, they need more time to develop the necessary competencies to work with HRM systems (Gardner, Lepak, & Bartol, 2003; Strohmeier, 2007). These changes justify an in-depth study about its impact in a medium term.

Many authors have also tried to study the specific impact of some areas of e-HRM, e-recruitment/e-selection being the most frequently studied. At this level, many studies suggest a considerable reduction of global costs due to the efficiency increase in recruitment and selection and to the (consequent) reduction of employee turnover and costs with personnel management processes (Buckley, Minette, Joy, & Michaels, 2004).

About e-HRM impact at the effectiveness level (namely, the quality of HR services), nevertheless the positive tendency, results are also hybrid and limited. Research shows that, generally, e-HRM helps enhance the capability of responding, in terms of information supply, to other organizational actors as well as improve technician autonomy in the management of this same information, allowing, at the same time, a great connection to specialist networks (Gardner et al., 2003).

Nevertheless, when e-recruitment results are specified, for instance, conclusions highlight advantages and disadvantages. Some studies suggest that although e-recruitment increases the number of vacancies, frequently, their quality is smaller (Chapman & Webster, 2003). Other studies suggest that online recruitment is globally more effective than any formal recruitment source (McManus & Ferguson, 2003). Others still call attention to some moderate variables of the relation between online job vacancies and recruitment process quality (i.e., candidate qualification and its alignment or fit with the function open), namely, the type of job portal where the vacancy is announced, since specialized portals seem to guarantee better results (Jattuso & Sinar, 2003).

In what concerns the potential segregationist or discriminatory effect of online recruitment (supposedly a limitation to job offers access to some minorities), some studies show that when compared with other formal recruitment sources, e-recruitment seems to reach a large number of candidates belonging to minority groups (Chapman & Webster, 2003; McManus & Ferguson, 2003).

In sum, studies suggest an e-HRM positive impact at the level of the efficiency and effectiveness of HR processes, making more studies necessary, and with better quality, in order to defintely corroborate this relation.

Related to the e-HRM impact in HR policies and practice standardization and harmonization—and although it is understandable that the approach, through e-HRM, of geographically distant actors makes this task easy (Rüel et al., 2004)—what is true is that this subject has been neglected in scientific research (Strohmeier, 2007).

Last, empirical evidence about e-HRM transformational role has been scarce and inconclusive. Indeed, in 2007, Strohmeier proceeded to conduct a literature review about the subject, selecting 57 high-quality researches that had been conducted since 1995 and concluded that despite e-HRM transformational potential suggested by the studies, their results were not sufficiently robust and conclusive. Later, in 2013, Marler and Fisher analyzed 40 quality studies published between 1999 and 2011. From this analysis, they concluded that the empirical support to this e-HRM result is indeed small and limited. So from the 40 studies considered, only six specifically have tested this result, and none of them have used a research methodology that permits to derive the cause–effect relations between e-HRM implementation and HRM role transformation. But out of the six studies, only three were conducted at the organizational level, and only two of them found a positive relation between both variables. The remaining three studies were conducted at the individual level (i.e., they have analyzed the perception of the organizational actors about e-HRM) and have ascertained the different results to be inconclusive.

Nevertheless, it should be stressed that this does not mean that e-HRM does not have this transformational potential, but only that it is not yet promoted in most organizations. Releasing HR managers from administrative tasks (through process automation and the devolvement of some of these tasks), e-HRM established conditions for them in order to have more time to support strategic management decisions. Besides, as seen earlier, e-HRM allows HR professionals to easily communicate with all internal stakeholders and quickly produce detailed reports about relevant indicators at the HR level, which is indeed a very important source of information for top management and the decisions that they need to make. The only problem is that organizations have not yet taken advantage of this potentiality, despite the HRM strategic role being defended for decades by all authors of this research area.

Finally, considering that the aim of HRM will always be to contribute to organizational performance improvement, it will be relevant to understand in what way e-HRM makes it easier, or not, to obtain this aim. Nevertheless, and according to Marler and Fisher (2013), any research had studied, until today, the relationship between e-HRM implementation and organizational performance measures (namely, competitive advantage). Probably it is due to the difficulty not only in having access to the necessary information to this type of studies due to barriers put by organizations themselves (Marler & Fisher, 2013) but also in operationalizing variables involved in this relation, considering that many other factors besides HRM influence organizational performance, making it difficult to discriminate their independent effects.

In conclusion, we can consider that the e-HRM potential in HR process improvement is indeed undeniable; however, more studies with better quality are necessary in order to reach robust conclusions at this level and to define what moderate variables can influence results obtained with e-HRM, in order to derive an implementation model of e-HRM systems.

5.5   e-HRM in small- and medium-sized organizations: State of the art

Despite increased research in e-HRM in the last decades, few authors have studied this reality in SMEs.* However, some authors have included

---

* For the purpose of this chapter, we have considered the SME definition established in the European Commission Recommendation of May 6, 2003, according to which "1. SME category is constituted by organizations that employ less than 250 workers and whose annual business volume doesn't exceed 50 million euros, or whose total annual balance doesn't exceed 43 million euros. 2. In SME category, a small organization is defined as an organization that employs less than 50 workers and whose annual business volume or total annual balance doesn't exceed 10 million euros. 3. In SME category, a micro organization is defined as an organization that employs less than 10 workers and whose annual business volume or total annual balance doesn't exceed 2 million euros" (p. L 124/39). With regard to the exploratory study (which is going to be presented in the next chapter) and considering that it will be difficult to obtain data regarding the business volume or total annual balance, we will consider only the criterion of the workers' number in order to classify the studied organizations.

the variable "organizational dimension" in their studies about e-HRM, which can offer some interesting indicators. At this stage, it should be pointed out that the SME definition used in these studies does not correspond to the definition used in this chapter, since they consider SME organizations with less than 500 workers (and not 250, as we consider in this chapter).

In general, and as expected, different studies have shown that large organizations greatly use HRM new technologies than SMEs (Ball, 2001; Strohmeier & Kabst, 2009). However, it is possible for this tendency to start reversing. Indeed, organizations that develop HR software not only present more and more solutions directed to SMEs' needs and financial capacity, but HR process outsourcing also seems to be a way for SMEs to implement e-HRM without doing high investment (Keebler, 2001, quoted by Strohmeier & Kabst, 2009).

On the other hand, some other studies suggest a different use of e-HRM for SMEs and large organizations (Ball, 2001; Hussain, Wallace, & Cornelius, 2007). More specifically, Hussain et al. (2007) showed that e-HRM uptake in areas such as salary processing, benefits management, and recruitment was significantly higher in large organizations than in SMEs. No significant differences were observed in the areas of HR planning, industrial relations, training, and performance management. In the same vein, another study, conducted in 2004, in Canada, showed that when compared with SMEs, large organizations frequently had more corporative websites and gave greater consideration to online recruiters (Hausdorf & Duncan, 2004).

The only two descriptive studies about e-HRM, specifically in SMEs, which was possible for us to find, were conducted in Malaysia. In one of them, directed specifically to e-recruitment, authors have concluded that in this country, SME e-recruitment was still incipient, not being practically used, even by the largest recruitment organizations (Poorangi, Khin, & Rahmani, 2011). In the other, more global study authors observed that the majority of SMEs continued to pursue conventional HRM, justifying this with the lack of financial resources, knowledge, or infrastructures adequate to e-HRM implementation. Besides, communication and salary processing were the most used e-HRM areas, considering that most organizations (56.7%) develop salary processing electronically, 80% had a corporate website, and 58.4% had an intranet available to all employees (Hooi, 2006).

In Portugal, a recent study about e-recruitment in the Minho region organizations provided some interesting indicators about the use of e-HRM. Among the SMEs analyzed in this study ($N = 13$), 69% promoted their job vacancies online, although from these only 15% use their own website. Social network use was a regular practice in 23% of the studied SMEs (Rodrigues, 2014).

5.6   e-HRM in SMEs of a particular region (Esposende) at the north of Portugal: An exploratory study

5.6.1   Some methodological and characterization elements

Considering the (almost) nonexistence of data about e-HRM in Portugal, an exploratory study about this reality in a particular region (Esposende municipality) was developed, justifying this option as it was easier to contact the organizations of this region (a convenience sample was used). Conscious of the impossibility of obtaining representative and generalizable data, the study only looks to characterize, in a brief way, e-HRM practices in a region where, like in all countries, almost all the existent organizations are SMEs.

Data were obtained through a questionnaire, designed intentionally to the effect and answered online as well as "in paper" by HR managers/other managers of the studied organizations. First, the organizations were contacted directly by the researchers, who asked for their collaboration in the study, and second, through e-mail, in those situations where the questionnaire was not answered at the moment. From the 24 contacted organizations, 12 accepted to collaborate in the study, which implies a reply rate of 50%.

Concerning organization characterization, it is important that these organizations belong to different activity sectors, from retail to commerce, passing through health care and social area and the textile, mechanics, wood, electricity, plumbing, and aluminum industries. On average, these organizations have 16.9 activity years, and regarding its dimension, half of them ($N = 6$) are small organizations, 41.7% ($N = 5$) are medium organizations, and 8.3% ($N = 1$) are micro organizations. Only four (33.3%) of these organizations have an HR department, considering that in the other situations, HRM tasks are assumed by someone in the administration ($N = 1$), assumed by someone specially employed for HRM ($N = 1$), or shared by different people, internal or external to the organization (namely, accounting, management) ($N = 6$).

In what concerns the functions performed by those who have answered the questionnaires, there were four HR managers, two HR technicians, three administrative technicians, one general manager/ administrator, and two financial managers.

5.6.2   Main result analysis

Analyzing the results as a whole, we can say that e-HRM, in the studied SMEs, is more intensively used in the administrative, communication, and recruitment areas.

So regarding administrative tasks, the results show that the five medium organizations of the study (41.7%) use a specific software for tasks such as hourly register and management, presences, absences, and holidays or official map production. Other functionalities of this software are function description, elaboration/actualization (used by four organizations), and the register of task production/realization times (used by three organizations). Concerning the organizations that do not have at one's disposal any software, specific to the HR area, a majority of tasks are developed utilizing MS Office (e.g., Word, Excel).

At the communication level, all organizations use the telephone or mobile phone for internal and external communication, 91.7% ($N = 11$) make use of e-mail, and 25% ($N = 3$) use Skype. Only one organization does not have its own website. The majority (66.7%; $N = 8$) is represented in Facebook, 8.31% ($N = 1$) in LinkedIn, an equal percentage in Twitter, 16.7% ($N = 2$) in Instagram, and 33.3% ($N = 4$) is not present in any social network. Five organizations (41.7%)—two small and the other three of medium dimension—dispose of one internal network/intranet, but in three of them (60%), this internal network is only available to the administration and offices/departments and not to the employees in general. In the intranet, the kind of information available to be consulted include employee personal and professional data ($N = 2$); the organization welcome and integration manual ($N = 2$); function description/competence profile ($N = 1$); holidays, absences, and schedules/shifts ($N = 3$); earnings receipts ($N = 1$); and/or benefits/incentives ($N = 1$). In two of those five organizations, some of this information (personal and professional data; competence profile; holidays, absences, and schedules/shifts; and fuel and meal expenses, for instance) can be consulted as well as edited/actualized.

In what concerns e-recruitment practices, half of the organizations say that they publish their job offers in websites/online job portals, 8.3% ($N = 1$) in their own website, equal percentage in specialized websites (e.g., professional associations), and 16.7% ($N = 2$) in social websites. A majority of the organizations (66.7%, $N = 8$) suggest in their job announcements that applications can be sent by e-mail. In none of them, the application submission online is allowed by their website.

Relating to the e-selection processes, two organizations prefer that they develop interviews via telephone and one of them also by videoconference. One of these organizations also conducts psychological tests or other tests of competence assessment online. Another organization disposes a software/informatics program that helps in curriculum vitae selection.

None of the studied organizations develop training needs identification through online, e-mail, or intranet questionnaires. Among the five organizations that develop internal training for their employees, only two of them (40%) have used e-learning (although rarely).

Finally, relating to the advantages of the new technologies' use in HRM, it is possible to highlight "the improvement in the quality of the developed work" and "the higher speed in task performance," which have been expressed by a majority of the organizations (66.7% and 58.3%, respectively). Only 33.3% (N = 4) pointed out as an advantage the fact that e-HRM releases HRM from more administrative tasks, making it possible to give more strategic support to management. With regard to disadvantages, the most signalized (by half of the organizations) was "the high financial investment necessary to introduce new technologies (e.g., intranet, software)." The fact that 25% (N = 3) of the respondents considered that e-HRM does not have any disadvantage is also highlighted.

In short, although not representative, these results are consistent with literature, as they point to a greater use of e-HRM in the administrative, communication, and recruitment areas. As a positive item, it is relevant to point out that the five medium-sized organizations have their own software, with diverse applications in the HR area, and five of the studied organizations (small and medium size) have at one's disposal the intranet. Nevertheless, considering that only two of them have the intranet available to consult or information edition by employees, allow us to conclude that it is still possible to maximize the potential of this tool at the organization service.

At the e-recruitment and e-selection level, considering that a majority of the organizations publish job offers online and suggest sending the curriculum vitae through e-mail, this procedure is a relevant signal, showing that even for SMEs, the Internet is nowadays a very common work tool. Also important to highlight is the fact that one of the organizations has a specific software for curriculum vitae selection, which could not be expected in an SME.

Also at the training level, it is possible to highlight that a majority of the organizations do not develop internal training, a reason why it is not surprising that only two (among those five that develop internal training) have used e-learning tools to implement training.

Finally, it is clear that the main e-HRM perceived advantage is HRM efficiency and effectiveness, with the e-HRM transformational role pointed out only by four respondents. These results are also coherent with the fact that although theoretically e-HRM can improve HRM strategic contribution to top management, in reality the organizations do not show clearly that this is so.

These results show that, although its dimension and its localization are in a small municipality, these SMEs highlight some relevant indices of e-HRM use. However, it is even possible to do more, and organizations could be more successful if they invest in the creation of this kind of resources. Indeed, the use of specific software in the HR area or the implementation of an internal website will probably imply costs that these organizations were not able to support at the moment. Effectively, high costs are indeed the main disadvantage pointed out by respondents. However, there are some free tools that organizations could use in order to make internal communication easier, increase employee commitment, and free the HR department from more administrative tasks, namely, tools that allow the document division and online edition (the so-called clouds), inclusive of more than one employee simultaneously, according to the use of a user account, created freely to the effect.

5.7   Final remarks

This chapter provided knowledge of some of the technological tools that HRM has nowadays in order to carry out their day-to-day tasks. The use of e-mail or videoconference, e-recruitment, or e-learning is very familiar to us, but the same cannot be said about the several informatics software functionalities or enterprise resources planning (ERPs) that exist today in the HR area.

Beyond that, it was also relevant to understand that in many of these organizations, particularly with smaller dimensions, HRM is still very devalued, considered as a synonym of salary processing and absence control and, in this way, seen as a task that inevitably is up to the accountant and top management.

References

Ball, K. S. The use of human resource information systems: A survey. *Personnel Review*, 30 (6) (2001): 677–693.

Bondarouk, T., & Ruël, H. The strategic value of e-HRM: Results from an exploratory study in a governmental organization. *The International Journal of Human Resource Management*, 24 (2) (2013): 391–414.

Bondarouk, T., Rüel, H., & Van der Heijden, B. e-HRM Effectiveness in a Public Sector Organization: A multi-stakeholder perspective. *International Journal of Human Resource Management*, 20 (3) (2009): 578–590.

Buckley, P., Minette, K., Joy, D., & Michaelis, J. The use of an automated employment recruiting and screening system for temporary professional employees: A case study. *Human Resource Management*, 43 (2/3) (2004): 233–241.

Chakraborty, A. R., & Mansor, N. N. A. Adoption of human resource information system: A theoretical analysis—2nd International Conference on Leadership, Technology and Innovation Management. *Procedia—Social and Behavioral Sciences*, 75 (2013): 473–478.

Chapman, D. S., & Webster, J. The use of technologies in the recruiting, screening, and selection processes for job candidates. *International Journal of Selection and Assessment*, 11 (2/3) (2003): 113–120.

Comissão Europeia. *Recomendação da Comissão de 6 de Maio de 2003 relativa à definição de micro, pequenas e médias empresas* (2003/361/CE). Accessed on May 17, 2015 at http://eur-lex.europa.eu/legal-content/PT/TXT/PDF/?uri=CELEX:32003H0361&from=EN, 2003.

Derouin, R. E., Fritzsche, B. A., & Salas, E. E-learning in organizations. *Journal of Management*, 31 (6) (2005): 920–940.

Dery, K., Grant, D., & Wiblen, S. *Human resource information systems (HRIS): Replacing or enhancing HRM*. Paper presented at the Proceedings of the 15th World Congress of the International Industrial Relations Association, IIRA 2009, Sydney, August 27, 2009).

De Sanctis, G. Human resource information systems: A current assessment. *Management Information Systems Quarterly*, 10 (1) (1986): 15–27.

Eckhardt, A., Laumer, S., Maier, C., & Weitzel, T. The transformation of people, processes, and IT in e-recruiting. *Employee Relations*, 36 (4) (2014): 415–431.

Ensher, E. A., Nielson, T. R., & Grant-Vallone, E. Tales from the hiring line: Effects of the internet and technology on HR processes. *Organizational Dynamics*, 31 (3) (2002): 224–244.

Furtmueller, E., Wilderom, C., & Tate, M. Managing recruitment and selection in the digital age: e-HRM and resumes. *Human Systems Management*, 30 (2011): 243–259.

Galanaki, E. The decision to recruit online: A descriptive study. *Career Development International*, 7 (4) (2002): 243–251.

Gardner, S. D., Lepak, D. P., & Bartol, K. M. Virtual HR: The impact of information technology on the human resource professional. *Journal of Vocational Behavior*, 63 (2) (2003): 159–179.

Haines, V. Y., & Petit, A. Conditions for successful human resource information systems. *Human Resource Management*, 36 (2) (1997): 261–275.

Hausdorf, P. A., & Duncan, D. Firm size and internet recruiting in Canada: A preliminary investigation. *Journal of Small Business Management*, 42 (3) (2004): 325–334.

Hooi, L. W. Implementing e-HRM: The readiness of small and medium sized manufacturing companies in Malaysia. *Asia Pacific Business Review*, 12 (4) (2006): 465–485.

Huselid, M. A. Editor's note: Special issue on e-HR—The intersection of information technology and human resource management. *Human Resource Management*, 43 (2/3) (2004): 119.

Hussain, Z., Wallace, J., & Cornelius, N. The use and impact of human resource information systems on human resource management professionals. *Information & Management*, 44 (2007): 74–89.

Instituto Nacional de Estatística. *Inquérito à Utilização de Tecnologias de Informação e Comunicação pelas Famílias*. Accessed on May 12, 2015 at https://www.ine.pt/xportal/xmain?xpid=INE&xpgid=ine_indicadores&indOcorrCod=0006679&contexto=bd&selTab=tab2, 2014.

Jattuso, M. L., & Sinar, E. F. Source effects in internet-based screening procedures. *International Journal of Selection and Assessment*, 11 (2/3) (2003): 137–140.

Leal, D., & Amaral, L. *Do ensino em sala ao e-Learning*. Accessed on May 10, 2015 at http://www.campusvirtual.uminho.pt/uploads/celda_av04.pdf, 2006.

Lee, I. The architecture for a next-generation holistic E-recruiting system. *Communications of the ACM*, 50 (7) (2007): 81–85.

Lengnick-Hall, M., & Mortiz, S. The impact of e-HR on the human resource management function. *Journal of Labor Research*, 24 (3) (2003): 365–379.

Lepak, D. P., & Snell, S. A. Virtual HR: Strategic human resource management in the 21st century. *Human Resource Management Review*, 8 (3) (1998): 215–234.

Marler, J. H. Making human resources strategic by going to the Net: Reality or myth? *The International Journal of Human Resource Management*, 20 (3) (2009): 515–526.

Marler, J. H., & Fisher, S. L. An evidence-based review of e-HRM and strategic human resource management. *Human Resource Management Review*, 23 (1) (2013): 18–36.

McClelland, S. B. Training needs assessment data-gathering methods: Part 1, survey questionnaires. *Journal of European Industrial Training*, 18 (1) (1994): 22–26.

McManus, M. A., & Ferguson, M. W. Biodata, personality, and demographic differences of recruits form three sources. *International Journal of Selection and Assessment*, 11 (2/3) (2003): 175–183.

Nesbeitt, S. L. Trends in internet-based library recruitment. *Internet Reference Services Quarterly*, 4 (2) (1999): 23–40.

Ngai, E. W. T., & Wat, F. K. T. Human resource information systems: A review and empirical analysis. *Personnel Review*, 35 (3) (2006): 297–314.

Panayotopoulou, L., Vakola, M., & Galanaki, E. E-HR adoption and the role of HRM: Evidence from Greece. *Personnel Review*, 36 (2) (2007): 277–294.

Parry, E., & Tyson, S. Desired goals and actual outcomes of e-HRM. *Human Resource Management Journal*, 21 (3) (2011): 335–354.

Poorangi, M. M., Khin, E. W. S., & Rahmani, N. SMEs portfolio of e-recruitment: Malaysian perspective. *International Journal of e-Education, e-Business, e-Management and e-Learning*, 1 (4) (2011): 332–337.

Rodrigues, R. *E-recrutamento como opção estratégica: realidade ou quimera nas empresas da região Minho?* Dissertação de Mestrado em Gestão de Recursos Humanos. Braga, Portugal: Escola de Economia e Gestão da Universidade do Minho, 2014.

Ruël, H. J. M., Bondarouk, T., & Looise, J. C. E-HRM: Innovation or irritation. An explorative empirical study in five large companies on web-based HRM. *Management Review*, 15 (3) (2004): 364–381.

Ruta, C. D. The application of change management theory to HR portal implementation in subsidiaries of multinational corporations. Human *Resource Management*, 44 (1) (2005): 35–53.

Stone, D. L., & Dulebohn, J. H. Emerging issues in theory and research on electronic human resource management (eHRM). *Human Resource Management Review*, 23 (2013): 1–5.

Strohmeier, S. Research in e-HRM: Review and implications. *Human Resource Management Review*, 17 (2007): 19–37.

Strohmeier, S. Assembling a big mosaic—A review of recent books on electronic human resource management (e-HRM). *German Journal of Research in Human Resource Management*, 26 (3) (2012): 282–294.

Strohmeier, S., Kabst, R. Organizational adoption of e-HRM in Europe: An empirical exploration of major adoption factors. *Journal of Managerial Psychology*, 24 (6) (2009): 482–501.

chapter six

Collaboration in processes supported by Web 2.0
The emergence of interactivity

*Jorge da Silva Correia-Neto, Jairo Simião Dornelas,
and Catarina Rosa e Silva de Albuquerque*

Contents

Abstract

Social platforms based on Web 2.0 have become of great interest to organizations, communities, and individuals with their capacity to increase
collaboration, sharing, and interactivity. These social platforms have
been used in both marketing and innovation, but more specifically in

open innovation, where research and development open up to the existent knowledge outside the walls of the organization. However, since the traditional models of collaboration mediated by technology are from the 1990s, this research has studied the platforms based on Web 2.0, which are used in the processes of open innovation, reflecting upon the underlying models that outline these collaborative systems under the lens of adaptive structuration and social exchange theories (AST and SET). Through a qualitative study of exploratory–descriptive nature, data were obtained from two case studies, one in the Brazilian subsidiary of Fiat and another in the United States at Local Motors. Platform functionality analyses and content analysis of the interviews with creators and developers, as well as direct observation, were done. Systematic mapping was also made, searching for models and conceptual references that would firmly consolidate the proposition of an interactive collaboration model. As a result, the communication, coordination, and cooperation dimensions present in the traditional 3C collaboration model were confirmed, but the interactivity dimension has also emerged. The i3C interactive collaboration model proposed is an academic contribution and also a contribution to the industry.

Keywords: Collaboration, Open innovation, Interactivity, 3C model, Web 2.0

6.1   Introduction

Since the beginning, platforms and social network sites based on the Internet have become of great interest to organizations, communities, and individuals for their capacity of easing collaboration, sharing, and interaction (Alberghini et al., 2014; Cheung and Lee, 2010), specially for being part of what is known as Web 2.0, or social web, which emphasizes user-generated content, produced in a collaborative manner (O'Reilly, 2005).

In this new universe powered by Web 2.0, as Vreede et al. (2009, p. 121) emphasized, collaboration became "a critical phenomenon in organizational life." Therefore, many organizations have already started to appropriate the social network dynamics to increase the synergy among their workers (Correia-Neto et al., 2011) and among business partners (Orlikowski and Woerner, 2009), in other words, intra- and interorganizational ramifications.

Thereby, it became strategic to organizations to appropriate that social logic and bring potential clients to collaborate in cocreation, coproduction, and distribution of goods, strengthening connections between clients and companies (Orlikowski and Thompson, 2010). It is also important to point out that cocreation and coproduction are part of the open innovation organizational process, which starts from the idea that there is much knowledge available beyond the walls of the organization and many people are interested in collaborating, including through the web (Chesbrough, 2003; Ramaswamy and Gouillart, 2010).

In this more social and interactive context, there come challenges to the implementation and usage of collaborative systems. When taking the systematic mapping of collaboration models mediated by technology, very few models, the most traditional, were identified; the 3C collaboration model (Fuks et al., 2008) was based on the propositions of Ellis et al. (1991), and the following research question emerged: Which dimensions must a collaboration model contain to handle this more social and interactive universe that came with Web 2.0?

The literature review pointed out that there are no guidelines or templates for the design of collaborative systems regarding collaboration in processes supported by information technology, or these guidelines are still based on the original web. Consequently, this research had as a general objective to propose an interactive collaborative model supported by Web 2.0 in open innovation processes, taking as reference the 3C collaborative model and the emergency of interactivity based on more social aspects of technology usage.

To understand this proposition, this study brought to discussion the theories by the optics of structuration and social exchanges, the models of collaboration coming from the systematic mapping, and two case studies. Its plot is described in five sections, starting with this introduction. Section 6.2 does a literature review about the research topics. Section 6.3 reports the methodological procedures adopted. In Section 6.4, the results are presented and discussed, and in Section 6.5, the study conclusions are presented.

6.2   Literature review

This section has as objective to expose, in a very summarized way, the main concepts and theories used in this study.

6.2.1   Theories and organizational models by the structuration lens

The usage of organizational theories under the structuration lens in this study is justified by its processual and structural vision of the organization (Niederman et al., 2008, 2009); here considered strategic to the study of the appropriation, social actors make the platforms of virtual social networks.

Giddens (1976, p. 104) establishes that, in organizations, the social actors create and recreate three key elements of social interaction: "meaning, power, and rules," which, according to Pires (1999), indicate that the structure must be understood simultaneously as a condition and result of the action, as enabler and compeller of the actor's intervention.

In other words, the structure is always dual: it limits and makes possible human actions and is also shaped at the same time by it. Besides, systems are regular social relations established among actors, which consolidate over time.

Assuming that technology has its own structures, DeSanctis and Poole (1994) consider that social practices moderate the effect of these structures over the behavior of the people involved to the implementation of that technology. Thus, the AST "starts considering the mutual influence of technology and social processes" (DeSanctis and Poole, 1994, p. 125). On the other hand, the spirit of these technologies "is the general intent in relation to the underlying values and objectives to a given group of functionalities" (DeSanctis and Poole, 1994, p. 126), that is, values and intentions underlying the systems delivered to users.

The choice of these theories is due to the fact that these platforms are emergent, being adjusted as the community is being established, and the IT artifacts can be described as the technical objects with functional capabilities and symbolic expressions.

6.2.2 Social exchange theory

SET explains the social changes and stability as a process of negotiable trades between sides, both between and within groups. Questions of "structure, process and function, static of dynamic, find their own place in this analytical scheme" of SET, says Merton (1950, p. xxi).

To Homans (1950), social exchanges are based on three elements: activities, which are tasks or operations done on a physical environment or over people; feelings, which are the act or effect of feeling something in relation to someone or something; and interactions, one's activities reflect upon another's and generate feelings between actors; they can motivate or demotivate the increase of frequency of these interactions.

At last, as said by Mogulof et al. (1964), in the homansian vision, groups are social systems that adapt to the environment and, at the same time, modify it due to their interdependency.

Besides the exchange process as a central element of SET, Homans (1958) points out three other elements. The first is the influence process, with the cohesion and interaction variables. Cohesion is a value variable that measures how much something attracts people to be part of a group. Interaction is a frequency variable that measures the frequency of verbal behavior emission. So the more cohesive a group is, the more valuable will the exchange activity be and the bigger the average frequency of member interaction as well. Moreover, a big cohesion in the group eases the uniformization of behaviors in the direction of making these activities more valuable and repaying these activities with the same intensity. The second is practical balance, as actors are always making these exchanges in pursuit of balancing their gains and losses. The last element of this theory concerns the costs and is a complex relation of knowledge increase and adjustment in the work coordination of group members.

6.2.3   Collaborative systems

The study about collaborative tools supported by IT started in the twentieth century. Candotti and Hoppen (1999) had already spoken about collaboration, but guided by the model of Ellis et al. (1991), pointing cooperation as being formed by communication, coordination, and collaboration. It was from Fuks et al. (2003) that collaboration turned to be the main construct, containing the dimensions of communication, coordination, and cooperation, configuring the base to the design of the collaborative systems by Fuks et al. (2007):

- *Coordination (with three variants)*: People coordination is related to communication and context, while resource coordination is about the shared environment where interactions occur; and task coordination consists of the management of interdependencies between necessary jobs to achieve a certain common objective.
- *Cooperation*: It defines how the group members cooperate, produce, manipulate, and organize information, building and refining objects cooperatively.
- *Communication*: It involves the media to be transmitted, the way it is to be transmitted, the restriction access policies, the metainformation, and the conversation structure.

It is still worth mentioning that, to strengthen this kind of system, it has to bring closer the technical and the social (Koch, 2008), since Web 2.0 and Internet mobility increased the interactivity between users and system, broadening the possibilities of its functional approaches and arrangements (Zwass, 2014).

6.2.4   Collaboration

Collaboration is a multidimensional polysemic construct (Henneman et al., 1995), but as Denise (1990) says, it is different from communication because instead of a simple exchange of information, there is indeed the usage of information for something new to be created; from coordination because instead of a structural harmony, divergent insights and spontaneity are pursued; and from cooperation because it blossoms in the differences and requires disagreements.

Collaboration may be viewed in an affective (Lepper and Whitmore, 1996), sociological (Mattessich et al., 2001), or cognitive (O'dea et al., 2007) perspective but always seeking to increase the commitment between the actors and the objects in the quest for the results the group aim at, through artifacts that are more interactive (Ramaswamy and Gouillart, 2010).

Therefore, coordination is related to efficiency, to doing planned activities at a definite pace (Denise, 1990), outlining the necessary procedures and tasks to fulfill objectives, and synchronizing contributions from everyone to reach the desirable product or comprehension (Noble et al., 2001).

Cooperation is the "action or process of working together focusing on the same objective" (OD, 2011, online). It is a functional system of activities between two or more people, originating from an individual need to fulfill objectives in a multifaceted system (Barnard, 1979).

Communication, especially the one mediated by the computer (CMC), "created new social interaction possibilities, e.g. asynchronicity, absence of face-to-face interaction, anonymity, privacy, continuous contact with interlocutors always connected online and virtual communities," characterizing the twenty-first century with the mark of decentralized communication and with the creation of content by users through social media and social network, as defined by Pimentel et al. (2011, p. 66).

Interactivity "is that communication resource, mean, or process which allows the receptor to actively interact with the transmitter," while "[inter + action] is the action which is mutually performed by two or more things or two or more people," says Ferreira (2010, p. 484). Silva (2001, p. 13) even declares that informatics interactivity created a new communicational form where the message is editable, as far as it answers the requests of the one who consults, explores, and manipulates it. In this context, the sender builds a network of territories to explore and the receiver manipulates the message as a coauthor, true conceptor, reinforcing the meaning of "participation, intervention, bi-directionality, and multiplicity of connections."

With this brief literature review, it is necessary to indicate that the lenses of the theories pointed as encouragers of research structuring align the concepts about collaboration in environments that are equivalent to collaborative systems and cover the operational incursion in the field in searching for dimensions that are shaped from the 3C model in the Web 2.0 scope, a new glimpse on collaboration.

6.2.5   Categories of analyses

In a few words, Tables 6.1 through 6.4 present the properties of each one of the analyses' categories, the operational definition that guided the process of content analysis and the literature basis used to build this operational definition.

Table 6.1 Properties, concepts, and dimensions of the communication category

Category: Communication			
Properties/ labels	Operational definition	Literary base	Dimension properties
Source of information	Source of information.	Bordewijk and Van Kaam (1986)	High (+): at the individual's hands
		McMillan (2002)	Low (−): centralized
Time and subject	Individuals choose with whom, when, where, and what to talk.	Bordewijk and Van Kaam (1986)	High (+): at the individual's hands
		McMillan (2002)	Low (−): centralized
Communication direction	Communication direction.	Tapiador et al. (2006)	High (+): two-way Low (−): one-way
Communication objectives	Understanding the communication goal.	Grunig and Grunig (1989)	High (+): symmetric
		McMillan (2002)	Low (−): asymmetrical

Source: Literature and data analysis.

6.3   *Methodological procedures*

The research adopted a qualitative approach, given the nature of the social phenomena studied and the sense that people attach to what they talk and do (Richardson, 1999), of exploratory–descriptive character, to deepen the knowledge about the topic (Churchill, 1979) and detail its constitutive characteristics (Gil, 1999), with the strategy of case studies (Yin, 2010).

We choose two car manufacturers as case studies based on Stake's (1994) and Miles and Huberman´s (1994) propositions about instrumental cases and about a suitable, favorable and accessible environment to the study. Additionally, two case studies would contribute to generate a more solid knowledge basis (Yin, 2010).

The first phase of this research involved the systematic mapping of collaboration models in the five main research bases of computer science and business administration areas, following the orientations of Biolchini et al. (2005) and the object of another publishing, the case selection and confirmation of authorizations for the execution of the research, the identification of the people to be interviewed, and the construction of a research protocol, including the construction and validation of the inter-view script.

Table 6.2 Properties, concepts, and dimensions of the interactivity category

Category: Interactivity			
Properties/ labels	Operational definition	Literary base	Dimension properties
Influence	Reciprocal action or interplay.	OD (2011)	High (+): mutual Low (−): few
Resources	Means or process that allows the receiver to actively interact with the sender, mediated by the graphic interface.	Lemos (2000) Ferreira (2010)	High (+): some Low (−): few
Message mutability	Participatory production, where the sender is a potential receiver and the receiver is a potential sender.	Trivinho (1998) Silva (2001)	High (+): allow Low (−): do not allow
Sensory immersion	Allows to act within a representation to the actions varying with each interactive session.	Silva (2001)	High (+): allow Low (−): do not allow
Gradation	Degree of object manipulation.	Silva (2001)	High (+): can manipulate Low (−): has access only
Hierarchy	Includes human capabilities and its form of social interaction.	Silva (2001)	High (+): regulate collaboration Low (−): instrumentalize collaboration
Interaction direction	Interactions occur in a one-way or two-way manner.	McMillan (2002)	High (+): two-way; individual high control
Individual control level	The sense of control of the interactions is in the hands of the participants so that they have interchangeable roles.	McMillan (2002)	Low (−): one-way; individual low control

Source: Literature and data analysis.

The second phase involved the documental rising (collection and register of used videos and collaboration functionalities available through platforms)—the execution and transcription of interviews with people directly connected to the creation and development of the collaboration platforms.

Table 6.3 Properties, concepts, and dimensions of the cooperation category

Category: Cooperation			
Properties/ labels	Operational definition	Literary base	Dimension properties
Social situation	Type of relationship between the objectives of the actors in a given social situation	Deutsch (1949, 2006)	Strong (+): cooperative Low (−): competitive
Interdependence of goal awareness	Way to understand the interdependence of goals	Tjosvold (1984)	High (+): explicit Low (−): implicit
Goal dynamic	Deployment of interdependence dynamics of cooperation and competition	Tjosvold (1984)	High (+): positive cooperation Low (−): competition, individualism
Goal transparency	Activity's goal explanation	Lepper and Whitmore (1996)	High (+): explicit Low (−): implicit
Way of control	Activity control mechanisms	Procópio (2006)	High (+): rational Low (−): social

Source: Literature and data analysis.

The third phase performed three tasks. The first one was the analysis of the existing functionalities of the platforms, detailed in another publication, that using a "use case diagram" identified six and eleven collaborative functionalities at Fiat and Local Motors´ platforms, respectively. The second one was the analysis of videos posted, the observations performed and of the interviews collected. Analyzing the videos it was possible to find out the purpose of each of them, linking them to each of the platform's evolutionary stages. Analyzing the interviews, following the orientations of Bardin (1979) and using the Atlas.ti® software, it was possible to perform content analysis and to build graphics, associating categories and their properties or labels. Figure 6.1 summarizes this methodological path. The observations reinforced the content analysis. The third task was the proposition of the interactive collaboration model.

One of the studied cases was Fiat Mio's project, from the Brazilians' subsidiary of Fiat Motors, where Brondoni (2010) stresses the aspect of design of the third concept car of this automobile manufacturer, which involved thousands of collaborators through an Internet platform accessed from over 140 countries. Arruda et al. (2012) point out some numbers

Table 6.4 Properties, concepts, and dimensions of the coordination category

Category: Coordination			
Properties/ labels	Operational definition	Literary base	Dimension properties
Task interdependency	Pattern of relationships between tasks	McGrath et al. (2000)	High (+): greater interdependence Low (−): less interdependence
Process kind	Way from which participants learn with others; working from other's efforts	Lepper and Whitmore (1996)	High (+): established Low (−): emergent
Task complexity	Quantity and activities of flow control	Cardoso (2005)	High (+): lots Low (−): little amount
Type of interdependency of tasks	Way the activities interrelate	Malone (1990)	High (+): generic Low (−): specific
Goal	Delineation of necessary tasks and procedures	Noble et al. (2001)	High (+): explicit and shared Low (−): implicit and unshared
Time	Synchronization and meeting deadlines	Noble et al. (2001)	High (+): short and defined Low (−): flexible
Way of control	*Continuum* between spontaneous and coordination by a physical force	Lepper and Whitmore (1996)	High (+): coercive Low (−): spontaneous
Basic knowledge	Leveling that serves as the basis for group communication	Klein et al. (1999)	High (+): require Low (−): does not require
Mental model	Assumptions or methods defined and carried out by a group	Klein et al. (1999)	High (+): require Low (−): does not require
Alternative routines	Repertoire of routines to be used when the plan needs to be adjusted	Klein et al. (1999)	High (+): require Low (−): does not require
Knowledge of individual skills	Knowledge that levers and adjust the tasks	Klein et al. (1999)	High (+): require Low (−): does not require

(Continued)

Table 6.4 (Continued) Properties, concepts, and dimensions of the
coordination category

Category: Coordination			
Properties/ labels	Operational definition	Literary base	Dimension properties
Group type	Level of complexity evaluation, adaptability, and dynamics of the group	McGrath et al. (2000)	High (+): complex, dynamic, and adaptive Low (−): simple, static, and maladaptive

Source: Literature and data analysis.

related to the project: 1.5 million visitors to the project website and over 17,000 ideas and 3,000 sketches about propulsion, materials, safety, ergonomics, and design.

The Fiat Mio project started with an open TV call inviting everyone to think about how the car of the future should be. In 2009, there were no more sophisticated Web 2.0 platforms and the project's deadline was too short; Fiat used the WordPress® platform. In order to enhance interaction with the audience, 16 videos were posted on YouTube®, inviting Internet users to give ideas on the platform and showing every stage of the construction of the concept car that would be presented on "Salão do Automóvel" in 2010, in São Paulo.

The other case studied was Local Motors, an American vehicle manufacturer located in Arizona, pointed by Anderson (2010) as the most important at that time, as they were utilizing a collaborative Web 2.0 platform where over 20,000 designers, engineers, and enthusiasts developed vehicles together with the company's designers and engineers.

Founded in 2007, it had more than 60,000 followers on social networks and 35,000 engineers, designers, and enthusiasts contributing to the platform (Gastelu, 2013). As an example, the military vehicle Flypmode was developed by DARPA, in 2011, in less than 5 months and delivered in a ceremony with President Barack Obama.

Cruz (2014) also highlights the launch of the Strati, a car that has fairings, wheels, and several accessories printed in 3D at one go, in a partnership of Local Motors with two other companies.

The representativeness of the two cases is remarkable and makes possible, *en passant*, an idea of how important the evolution of a technology support is to the consolidation of an idea in an organizational scope, being, therefore, meritorious with the choices to study.

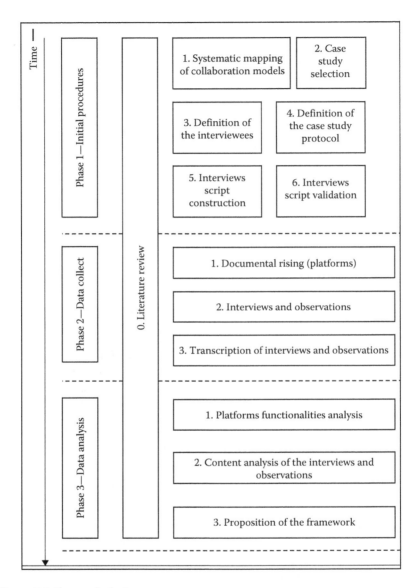

Figure 6.1 Research design.

6.4 Results

In this section, results are presented following the specific objectives set. A codification was used 'in text' for identification of transcription excerpts during analysis and discussion of findings. The third manager to be interviewed at Fiat was coded as FM3 and the third platform developer to be interviewed at Local Motors was coded as LMD3. The number that follows the comma was the paragraph of the interview transcription.

6.4.1   Pertinence of the 3C model

Aiming at evaluating the relevance of the 3C collaboration model as the analysis lens of platforms in Web 2.0, which is more social and with thousands of collaborators, a systematic mapping of collaboration models was made.

Automatic search tools brought up 724 articles, but after the application of inclusion and exclusion criteria, there were 14 selected articles with conceptual models of collaboration proposed, applied, or evaluated. Results ratify the relevance and pertinence of the 3C collaboration model to serve as scrutiny based on this very study. Besides the fact it shows up in many international studies in Portuguese language, the group of professors that thought about it, and uses it, has also produced significantly the collaborative systems theme.

6.4.2   Dimensions of collaboration mediated by
Web 2.0 technologies in the Fiat case

In the Fiat case, only three out of the four supposed dimensions were identified. The cooperation dimension was not identified, and perhaps this may be explained due to the fact that its platform had not made available functionalities that effectively lead to the construction of objects straight from collaborators nor existing interrelated and interdependent activities, as well as a sense of competition.

Data reveal that the coordination dimension was composed of the following properties: baseline knowledge, level of control, type of group, and objective, as shown in Figure 6.2.

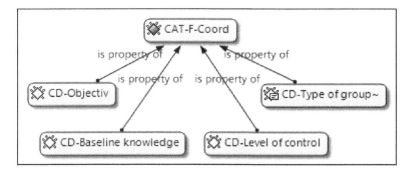

Figure 6.2 Coordination dimension on the Fiat case. (Extracted from Atlas.ti® on October 1, 2014.)

The baseline knowledge property evaluates if actions are performed to evaluate knowledge, searching for a minimal common understanding to the majority of participants, as in the following statement: "some inspiring posts we used to post daily and the objective of that was to level the group" (FM3, 7).

The level of control property evaluates if the coordination activity was done in the most pushed or spontaneous way, as in this statement: "we didn't need to remove participants, the community itself did the job of leaving out people who were not participating, not contributing with anything" (FM4, 6).

The type of group property indicates the level of complexity of the group formed around the platform, as the same respondent expressed: "every type of person participated in the project; there were children sending drawings, retired people and engineers who participated because they thought it was super interesting."

The objective property outlines the jobs and basic procedures, as in later on we had already set a target; we chose a certain topic, for instance, let's discuss how the shape of the steering wheel will be" (FM6, 2).

The communication dimension, as Figure 6.3 shows, had been presented to respondents, especially to empower two-way communication.

The communication direction property identified if this type of communication was effective between Fiat and its collaborators, as in "with the familiarity and socialization of Internet, this came to not only being just a conversation, but a chat" (FG4, 4).

The time and subject property evaluated if the choice of what and when to have a conversation was in the individual's hand, and not in

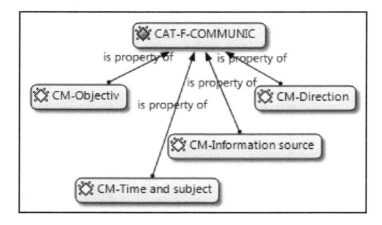

Figure 6.3 Communication dimension on the Fiat case. (Extracted from Atlas.ti® on October 1, 2014.)

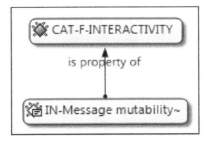

Figure 6.4 Interactivity dimension on the Fiat case. (Extracted from Atlas.ti® on October 1, 2014.)

the organization's. That aspect was evident in 11 quotes, one of which is "environment to free expression: was, especially because you can't control what's outside, but we already have this more open attitude, of free expression" (FG2, 16). However, it became evident that there was a different position from Fiat, because "every discussion we had on the website had to be directed" (FM6, 2), since the project was to develop the concept car.

The objective property seeks to evaluate if there was an understanding about the communication purpose, which became evident in statements like this: "there was a guy who said: 'I thought it was a joke, I didn't think they'd actually build the car. Build the car, listen to my ideas'" (FM4, 16).

As seen in Figure 6.4, the interactivity dimension was present in the Fiat case, even if incipiently, in the message mutability property, especially when it was articulated between the forum and the videos, even in a smaller gradation: "when people were going to post and saw the ideas had already been posted there, instead of reposting, they went there and talked over it, talked about their point of view" (FM4, 11).

At last, in the Fiat case, it is possible to highlight that to portray in a more complete way the phenomena of interactive collaboration, the coordination, communication, and interactivity dimensions were considered.

6.4.3   *Dimensions of collaboration mediated by Web 2.0 technologies in the Local Motors case*

In the Local Motors case, four supposed categories were identified, as summarized in Figures 6.5 through 6.8.

In the cooperation dimension, in the transparency of the activity objective property, the community managers absorbed the role of the leader and started identifying collaborators to each specific task, encouraging them, because they knew they were tailored for that mission.

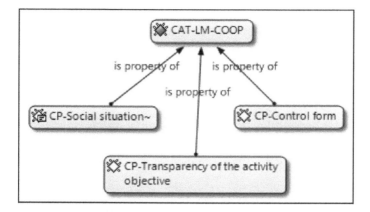

Figure 6.5 Cooperation dimension on the Local Motors case. (Extracted from Atlas.ti® on October 1, 2014.)

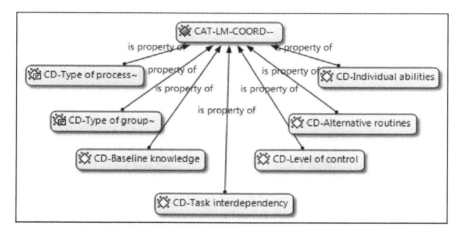

Figure 6.6 Coordination dimension on the Local Motors case. (Extracted from Atlas.ti® on October 1, 2014.)

In the control form property, two quotes stand out. The first comments that the platform provides version control for drawings and projects: "we have even version control" (LMD3, 19). And the second mentions the interest of the company in allowing the synchronous file edition, including CAD type: "ability to collaborate on CAD files is really the future" (LMD2, 4), reinforcing the need of a version control system, as suggested by McMillan (2002), reinforcing the high degree of control by the individual.

As an example of the property social situation, the Tandem project was analyzed. A collaborator had a Corolla engine and more than

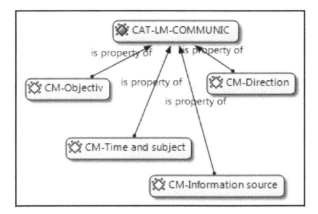

Figure 6.7 Communication dimension on the Local Motors case. (Extracted from Atlas.ti® on October 1, 2014.)

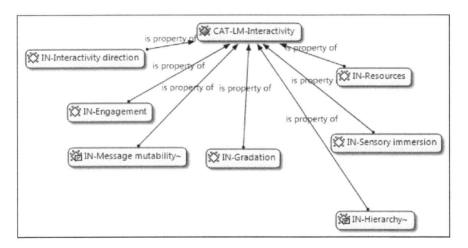

Figure 6.8 Interactivity dimension on the Local Motors case. (Extracted from Atlas.ti® on October 1, 2014.)

US$ 10,000 and wanted to gather a team that wanted to project and build a car for two people. That project quickly added many collaborators and was rapidly produced and everything was done collaboratively in a social and noncompetitive perspective, as pointed by Deutsch (2006).

The coordination dimension was present in the speech of the respondents of Local Motors, as shown in Figure 6.6.

The level of control property, as proposed by Lepper and Whitmore (1996), talks about the regulation used for the execution of a certain work, as said in the following quote: "they are self-regulating it" (LMG2, 17).

The type of group property shows the complexity of handling collaborators from different backgrounds that sometimes dedicate more, sometimes less, as shown in the following: "I like creating teams where everybody on the team is diverse in their background" (LMG1, 26). Obtaining commitment in these cases is only achieved through actions as the ones described in SET.

The task interdependency property, as proposed by McGrath et al. (2000), is a pattern of relationship between tasks, objectives, activities, and products, resulting from an emergent process in which the participants learn from one another and do their job with the effort of the others, as exemplified in the following: "we need this and this done, and there is the support material for that task, here is everything you need" (LMG1, 10).

The presence of the type of process property is also made clear in these lines: "you can find collectivist ways, but you ought to have clear problem statements and have a person that helps to steer the process" (LMG3, 9) and "there are lots of ways of using the platform" (LMD3, 24), where the alternative routines property is illustrated.

At its time, the baseline knowledge property, as proposed by Klein et al. (1999), evaluates if the basic information for the execution of a certain job are provided, as you can see in the following: "If you have a new tool you need to demonstrate and police how the new tool is being used, initially..." (LMG1, 8).

Finally, the individual abilities property involves the knowledge of how to leverage the completion of tasks as in "hey, you know about this thing; you are the right person for this project" (LMD3, 6).

The communication dimension is also presented, along with all its identified properties, summarized in Figure 6.7, especially in the sense of empowering two-sided communication. The line "a way to create conversation" (LMG4, 15) demonstrates that the direction property was redeemed in a visit to Local Motors. Other quotes also create a two-sided connection between collaborators and company: "the user voice pieces are really helpful for us to be able to develop the website as well" (LMG3, 19).

The time and subject property says that communication is two way and collaborators choose the topic, and at that moment, they decide to communicate and collaborate, as the following text fragment shows "sometimes those guys take their smartphones and film it, and take pictures, and so, it is definitely a collaborative effort" (LMG4, 6).

The information source property evaluates if it is centralized in the organization or spread, as shown in the following extract: "even people that we haven't been able to meet in person, know them in another way; oh, he is not active today because his mother got sick, and he is not able to interact today" (LMG2, 16).

Communication may have many objectives, but as pointed out by one of the respondents, "people want their opinion to be heard, and people want to share things" (LMG4, 10).

The interactivity dimension, shown in Figure 6.8, was the most high-lighted in the Local Motors case, showing seven properties and reinforc-ing the theoretic density factor, pointed out by Sherman and Webb (1988) as an import to make a theory more solid.

The resources used by Local Motors to amplify the interactivity of the platform with its collaborators were uncountable. We take the Tandem project as an example, where videos created by company workers them-selves showed parts of the vehicle under construction, as shown in the fol-lowing extract: "we work together, and sometimes those guys take their smartphones and film it, and take pictures, and so, it is definitely a col-laborative effort" (LMG4, 6).

The hierarchy property was present in the platform, but in a very accessible way, in fact, collaborators could post their ideas and projects in search of people interested to touch them in an open collaborative way, as in (LMD1, 8): "we have people actually bringing their own ideas."

The gradation property, according to Silva (2001), has in its highest level, the transformation of the manipulated objects, collaboratively. This is suggested at Local Motors in the following line: "does he take someone's idea and come up with his own spin on that idea? The answer is yes" (LMG1, 23).

The existence of the message mutability property was declared based on the interpretation of the following extracts: "joint ideas that is really the whole mind out there" (LMD3, 14) and "people can upload revisions to their project and communicate the direction the project is going visually" (LMG3, 17). This plot shows that interactivity is strong when a message is built by several hands, as preached by Silva (2001).

From the research objectives point of view, each and every collabora-tion dimension proposed by the 3C model and even more the interactivity dimension, shown initially as a hypothesis, was confirmed in the Local Motors case.

Communication was confirmed by conversations (texts, videos, etc.) executed daily among community members. Coordination was also con-firmed, because as there is much work being done in groups and inside the platform, functionalities to cover this demand are fundamental. Cooperation was also present along with the possibility of enlisting vol-unteers to run projects born in the community itself, such as the Tandem project. At last, the interactivity prompted by the tool and even the pres-ence of clients in the factory installations during the conclusion of its vehicles were points to highlight. Editing work projected by other com-munity members and developing them to new community iterations are examples of this interactivity strength in the platform.

Social Exchange Theory confirmed the usage of the platform to exchange experiences and acquire knowledge. Also, there was some kind of symbolic return in it, as in the case of the delivery of the DARPA project.

It has also been made clear that the usage of the theories under the optics of the structuration is appropriate to understand the platform evolution from the user communities' demands, in its three versions: the first focused on the designers, the second involving also engineers and the Rally Fighter car, and the third increasing the interactivity and making the user experience better.

6.4.4 Synthesis and cross analysis of the studied cases

The evidences collected at Fiat and Local Motors, based on elements brought by the software Atlas.ti, termed empirical groundedness and theoretic density, propitiates seeing, as summarized in Figure 6.9, that the four collaboration dimensions (from the 3C model and the study proposal) had backed up in the collected data in the form of interviews, especially communication and interactivity.

The level of empirical groundedness indicates the volume of quotes that proves the existence of that category, and in the studied cases, the volume was reasonable to the cooperation dimension and relevant to the other dimensions. In what concerns theoretic density, as said by Sherman and Webb (1988), to configure a more solid theory, it must have a few key elements and lots of properties and categories. With the executed content analysis, the statement that the collaboration construct has the three dimensions of the 3C model and also the dimension interactivity became ratified, strengthening it with the theoretic density of the four dimensions, especially the coordination and interactivity ones, which were present in the Local Motors case.

The functionality analysis of both platforms has shown that, while Fiat used the forum to let people criticize/contribute with previously posted ideas, textually, in Local Motors those critics/contributions could have been done in many ways and in several points of the platform. They could use a simple cool tag (positive), post a text/picture, share the idea on

Name	Grounded	Density
✖ CAT-General Communication	45	5
✖ CAT-General Cooperation	10	4
✖ CAT-General Coordination	33	8
✖ CAT-General Interactivity	70	7

Figure 6.9 Empirical groundedness and theoretic density of the collaboration construct. (Extracted from Atlas.ti® on October 1, 2014.)

social networks sites, or even download a shared file and upload it later with a contribution, such as the conversion of a drawing from 2D to 3D.

Anyway, with the cross analysis of functionalities, characteristics, categories, and conceptual dimensions present in both cases, it was possible to realize that these platforms are in a certain continuum, with Fiat on one side, with less interactivity and less collaborators, and with Local Motors on the other side, with more interactivity and less collaborators. A key point of this question seems to be that Local Motors has been investing in its platform since 2007, updating it to more complex and interactive collaborative contexts, such as the one used by General Electric company.

These impressions reinforced the thesis that in the design of collaborative platforms in Web 2.0 environments, there is something beyond the three original dimensions of the 3C collaboration model, being then admissible, the proposition of a new model that can handle this more social and interactive reality present in the collaborative platforms of Web 2.0. This very model is termed here as the i3C collaboration model and will be shown next.

6.5   Conclusions

Supporting the initial research vision regarding the need to update the 3C collaboration model, starting from a more interactive and social dynamic of Web 2.0, it was possible to ratify, as technology-mediated collaboration dimensions, communication, coordination, and cooperation and ratify the emergence of interactivity in this context.

Starting from the lenses of the AST, it became possible to see the evolution process of these platforms, the fruit of their users, and the different forms where they appropriate the technological tools. On the other hand, from the SET lenses, it was also possible to identify some of the main underlying motivations that cause millions of people to dedicate collaborative activities like the ones studied here.

Through existing functionality analysis in the studied collaborative platforms, it was possible to identify how their implementers enabled the construction of successful platforms, regardless of these platforms being supported by current technology, like Web 2.0, or less sophisticated tools, as it was in the Fiat case, with function aggregation.

To sum up, the summaries of the four identified dimensions and the proposition of a model with the rearrangement of these dimensions in the Web 2.0 context in open innovation processes are presented.

In relation to the communication dimension, analyzing the properties of information source control, time, and topic, according to McMillan (2002), it has been noticed that information sources are every time more decentralized and, the time and topic are defined by collaborators, making them important in this process, choosing with whom, when, where, and about what to talk. Still in the communication dimension, but under the optics of Grunig and Grunig (1989) and communication objectives, promoting a more conversational approach with their public, organizations should make two-way symmetric communication available.

In relation to the cooperation dimension, analyzing the question of the social situation, the relation between the studied social actors' objectives may be pointed clearly as cooperative. In what concerns the collaboration control format, it has been seen that it could come from the social environment or the individual's rational instrumental action (Procópio, 2006), but in the studied context, the social control mechanism was the most present one. When it comes to transparency, the actions willingly performed seek a common objective (Lepper and Whitmore, 1996), but in the studied context it has been done explicitly.

Moreover, concerning the coordination dimension, the baseline knowledge, individual's capacity knowledge, and alternative routines properties, as shown by Klein et al. (1999), involve the execution of a leveling, the knowledge of individual capacities, and the development of a repertoire of routines to be executed, which are all present in the studied context. In relation to the level of control property, pointed out by Lepper and Whitmore (1996) as a continuum between spontaneous coordination and coordination through a physical force, in this context it was spontaneous itself.

Still concerning the coordination dimension, for the type of process and task interdependency properties, following the thoughts of McGrath et al. (2000), the pattern of relationship between tasks, objectives, activities, and products, the result is an emergent process in which participants are continuously learning from one another and doing their job from everybody else's effort. Here, the interdependency between tasks is smaller and the process emergent.

At last, as closure of the coordination dimension, the type of group and objective properties were present, as foreseen by McGrath et al. (2000). It was also noticed that these groups perform tasks and procedures explicitly and implicitly in a defined and shared manner, as indicated by Noble et al. (2001).

In relation to the interactivity dimension, message mutability was seen, in the studied context, in both cases, exactly as seen by Silva (2001), that is, with conjoined production and participative production, where the sender is a potential receiver and the receiver is a potential sender. When it comes to the interaction direction and user control–level properties, McMillan (2002) says that, in the more advanced interactivity level, the mutual speech, there is a two-way communication and the control of this communicative experience is left in the hands of the receiver, which happened in this studied context.

As for the gradation property, Silva (2001) defines a continuum where the level is more advanced and is the one of continuous command, where there is transformation of manipulated objects, as what happens in Local Motors' collaborative platforms, since the objects can be manipulated by more than one person and there is still the intention of the company in installing the functionalities of version control of the objects posted in the environment.

In terms of hierarchy, Silva (2001) also states that interactivity can be seen in terms of its empirical or speculative form, though in the studied context it is speculative, via social interaction and regulation.

In relation to the resources made available, Lemos (2000) says that the more the interactivity resources in the collaborators' hand, the bigger their engagement. These resources also allow social immersion, with collaborators acting into a representation, with actions varying at each interactive section (Silva, 2001). Especially in the Local Motors platforms, these resources were made available in a bigger quantity and allowed a bigger social immersion since they aggregated expert and beginner pairs.

In this scope, interactivity inherent to Web 2.0 must be highlighted as a main innovative vector of the collaboration construct, an element that was not absorbed by the 3C model, which may be due to the time it was presented by Ellis et al. (1991).

Facing the obtained results and accomplished analysis, it is possible to state that the 3C model cannot conceptually cover all elements involved in the phenomena of collaboration in the interactive and social context of Web 2.0.

Furthermore, the interactive collaboration model, here termed the i3C model, exhibited in Figure 6.10, which was elaborated based on

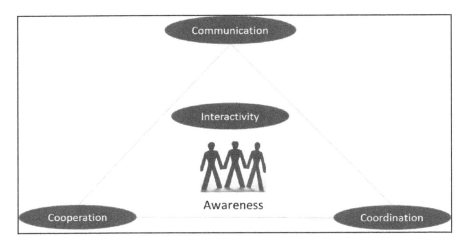

Figure 6.10 i3C collaboration model.

the analysis of the platform's functionalities, on on-site observations and on content analysis of the interviews with managers and platform developers, in the context of open innovation, is composed of four dimensions.

As a conclusion, with two field visits, with two instrumental cases, with distinct and complementary characteristics, and taking as the base the presented theoretical lenses, it was possible, with the help of the respondents, to unravel the new collaboration aspects that Web 2.0 tools support. From the data submitted for analysis, it has been possible to identify new and old categories and, after, put them in a new chain model of this construct.

The two field insertions served to reinforce the model built in the theoretical front, as data were collected and analyzed two times, in order to hoard emergent categories and confirm previously identified ones. These two field visits empowered the results, generating a model that is more effective to meet the validity and research reliability criteria.

To summarize, it may be checked in the present study that the 3C model is a solid one, but it needs to be updated to handle a phenomenon that has been transforming since the birth of social network platforms and, more recently, collaborative platforms that support open innovation, corroborating with the theoretical propositions that give foundation to the study.

As a main contribution to academics and to managers and developers, the following notion may be pointed out: in the design and implementation of collaborative systems, especially the ones used in open innovation processes, the principal focus of the artifact must be in the interactivity dimension, without leaving aside the communication, cooperation, and coordination dimensions and observing greater emphasis in the involved social aspects.

As examples of study limits, a short deadline used for collecting can be cast, which restrained a broader longitudinal vision and the fact that Fiat's respondents were talking about a project that happened between 2009 and 2010. Another limitation of this research was the fact that it could not have listened to the users' platforms, because other aspects, even more social ones, could have appeared. It is a side to be explored.

Last, the tackled theme in this research—collaboration models mediated by technology in the context of Web 2.0 and open innovation—is addressed very little in the literature, which made it difficult to compare with other studies. In fact, the collaboration topic mediated by technology is still incipient in conceptual scale and real practice.

In the future, the results and reflections raised from this study may broaden the knowledge about the usage of collaboration platforms in other organizational processes and may be used to validate the proposed model.

References

Alberghini, E., Cricelli, L., Grimaldi, M. A methodology to manage and monitor social media inside a company: A case study. *Journal of Knowledge Management*, 18 (2), 255–277, 2014.

Anderson, C. In the next industrial revolution, atoms are the new bits. Wired. January 25, 2010.

Arruda, C., Salum, B., Rennó, L. Caso de Inovação Fiat Automóveis—Estratégia de Inovação. Casos FDC. Nova Lima-MG, Brazil, 2012.

Bardin, L. *Análise de Conteúdo*. Lisboa, Portugal: Edições 70, 1979.

Barnard, C. *As funções do executivo*. São Paulo, Brazil: Atlas, 1979.

Biolchini, J., Mian, P. G., Natalli, A. C. C., Travassos, G. H. Systematic review in software engineering. Technical Report RT-ES 679/05, COPPE/UFRJ. 2005. Acesso em: 01 nov. 2012. Disponível em: http://alarcos.inf-cr.uclm.es/doc/MetoTecInfInf/Articulos/es67905.pdf.

Bordewijk, J. L., Van Kaam, B. Towards a new classification of tele-information services. *InterMedia*, 14 (1), 16–21, 1986.

Brondoni, S. M. Intangibles, global networks & corporate social responsibility. *Symphonya Emerging Issues in Management*, no. 2, 2010.

Candotti, C. T., Hoppen, N. Reunião Virtual e o uso de Groupware—uma nova possibilidade de realizar trabalho em grupo. Anais… In: *Encontro Nacional da ANPAD*, 1999, Foz do Iguaçu. Rio de Janeiro, Brazil: ANPAD, 1999, pp. 123–123.

Cardoso, J. Control-flow complexity measurement of processes and Weyuker's properties In: *Proceedings of the 6th International Enformatika Conference. Transactions on Enformatika, Systems Sciences and Engineering*, Budapest, Hungary, 8, 213–218, October 26–28, 2005.

Chesbrough, H. W. *Open Innovation: The New Imperative for Creating and Profiting from Technology*. Cambridge, MA: Harvard University Press, 2003.

Cheung, C. M. K., Lee, M. K. O. A theoretical model of intentional social action in online social networks. *Decision Support Systems*, 49 (1), 24–30, 2010.

Churchill, G. Paradigm for developing measures of marketing constructs. *Journal of Marketing Research*, 16, 64–73, February 1979.

Correia-Neto, J. S., Silva, A. A. B., Fonseca, D. Sites de Redes Sociais Corporativas: Entre o pessoal e o profissional. In: *III Encontro de Administração da Informação, 2011, Porto Alegre-RS*. Anais… Porto Alegre-RS, Brazil: UFRGS, 2011, 13pp.

Cruz, L. Local Motors lança primeiro carro impresso em 3D. Revista Exame. Acesso em: 20 set. 2014. Disponível em: http://exame.abril.com.br/estilo-de-vida/noticias/local-motors-lanca-primeiro-carro-impresso-em-3d.

Denise, L. Collaboration vs. C-Three. *Innovating* 7 (3), 1990. Accessed: 19 maio 2014. Available in: https://s3.amazonaws.com/KSPProd/cache/documents/646/64621.pdf.

DeSanctis, G., Poole, M. S. Capturing the complexity in advanced technology use: Adaptive structuration theory. *Organization Science*, 5 (2), 121–147, 1994.

Deutsch, M. A theory of co-operation and competition. *Human Relations*, 2, 129–152, 1949.

Deutsch, M. Cooperation and competition. In: Deutsch, M., Coleman, P. T., Marcus, E. C. (Eds.). *The Handbook of Conflict Resolution: Theory and Practice*. San Francisco, CA: Jossey-Bass, 2006.

Ellis, C. A., Gibbs, S. J., Rein, G. L. Groupware—Some issues and experiences. *Communications of the ACM*, 34 (1), 38–58, 1991.

Ferreira, A. B. H. *Mini Aurélio: o dicionário da língua portuguesa*, 8th ed. Curitiba, Brazil: Positivo, 2010.

Fuks, H., Raposo, A. B., Gerosa, M. A. Do Modelo de Colaboração 3C à Engenharia de Groupware. Anais... Simpósio Brasileiro de Sistemas Multimídia e Web—WebMídia 2003, Trilha Especial de Trabalho Cooperativo Assistido por Computador, Salvador, Brazil, 03 a 06 de Novembro de 2003, pp. 445–452.

Fuks, H., Raposo, A. B., Gerosa, M. A., Pimentel, M. The 3C collaboration model. In: Khosrow-Pour, M. (Ed.), *The Encyclopedia of E-Collaboration*, 2nd ed., 2008. Accessed: 15 Jan, 2011. Available in: http://www.groupwarework bench.org.br.

Fuks, H., Raposo, A. B., Gerosa, M. A., Pimentel, M., Filippo, D., Lucena, C. J. P. Inter- e Intra-relações entre Comunicação, Coordenação e Cooperação. In: *SBSC*, 27, 2007, Rio de Janeiro-RJ. Anais... Rio de Janeiro-RJ, Brazil, XXVII SBSC, 2007.

Gastelu, G. Local Motors partners with U.S. Army to bring crowdsourcing to the front lines. FoxNews.com. January 31, 2013.

Giddens, A. *New Rules of Sociological Method*. New York: Basic Books, 1976.

Grunig, J. E., Grunig, L. A. Toward a theory of public relations behavior of organizations: Review of a program of research. In: Grunig, J. E., Grunig, L. A. (Eds.). *Public Relations Research Annual*, Vol. 1, pp. 27–63. Hillsdale, NJ: Erlbaum, 1989.

Henneman, E. A., Lee, J. L., Cohen, J. L. Collaboration: A concept analysis. *Journal of Advanced Nursing*, 21 (1), 103–109, 1995.

Homans, G. C. *The Human Group*. New York: Harcourt, Brace and Company, 1950.

Homans, G. C. Social behavior as exchange. *American Journal of Sociology*, 63, 597–606, 1958.

Klein, G., Pliske, R., Wiggins, S., Thordsen, M. L., Green, S. L., Klinger, D., Serfaty, D. A model of distributed team performance. Final Report Contract N61339-98-C-0062 for NAWCTSD. Fairborn, OH: Klein Associates Inc., 1999.

Koch, M. CSCW and enterprise 2.0: Towards an integrated perspective. *Proceedings of the 21st Bled eConference*. Bled, Slovenia, 2008. Accessed: 10 set. 2014. Available in: http://aisel.aisnet.org/bled2008/15/.

Lemos, A. Anjos interativos e retribalização do mundo: Sobre interatividade e interfaces digitais. Acesso em: 02/05/2013. Disponível em: http://www.facom. ufba.br/ciberpesquisa/lemos/interac.html.

Lepper, M. R., Whitmore, P. Collaboration: A social-psychological perspective. *Cognitive Studies: The Bulletin of the Japanese Cognitive Science Society*, 3, 7–10, 1996.

Malone, T. W., Crowston, K. What is coordination theory and how can it help design cooperative work systems? In: *CSCW '90 Proceedings of the 1990 ACM Conference on Computer-Supported Cooperative Work*, pp. 357–370, 1990.

Mattessich, P. W., Murray-Close, M., Monsey, B. R. *Collaboration: What Makes It Work*, 2nd ed. Saint Paul, MN: Amherst H. Wilder Foundation, 2001.

McGrath, J. E., Arrow, H., Berdahl, J. L. The study of groups: Past, present, and future. *Personality and Social Psychology Review*, 4 (1), 95–105, 2000.

McMillan, S. J. A four-part model of cyber-interactivity: Some cyber-places are more interactive than others. *New Media Society*, 4 (2), 271–291, 2002.

Merton, R. K. Introduction. In: Homans, G. C. (Ed.), *The Human Group*. New York: Harcourt, Brace and Company, 1950.

Miles, M. B., Huberman, A. M. *Qualitative Data Analysis: An Expanded Sourcebook*, 2nd ed. Thousand Oaks, CA: Sage Publications, 1994.

Mogulof, M. B., French, D. G., Bloksberg, L. M., Stern, W. F. Homans' theory of the human group: Applications to problems of administration, policy, and staff training in group service agencies. *Journal of Jewish Communal Service*, 40 (4), 379–395, Summer 1964.

Niederman, F., Briggs, R. O., Vreede, G. J., Kolfschoten, G. L. Extending the contextual and organizational elements of Adaptive Structuration Theory in GSS. *Journal of the Association for Information Systems*, 9 (10/11), 633–652, 2008.

Niederman, F., Gregor, S., Grover, V., Lyytinen, K., Saunders, C. ICIS 2008 Panel report: IS has outgrown the need for reference discipline theories, or has it? *Communications of the Association for Information Systems*, 24, article 37, 2009. Available at: http://aisel.aisnet.org/cais/vol24/iss1/37.

Noble, D., Buck, D., Yeargain, J. Metrics for evaluation of cognitive-based collaboration tools. In: *Proceedings of the sixth ICCRTS Conference*, Annapolis, MD, 2001.

Orlikowski, W. J., Thompson, S. Leveraging social media for customer engagement: An experiment at BT. *CISR MIT Sloan Research Briefings*, X (4), 2010.

Orlikowski, W. J., Woerner, S. L. Web 2.0: Experimenting with the connected web. *CISR MIT Sloan Research Briefing*, IX (3), 2009. http://cisr.mit.edu/blog/documents/2009/05/29/2009_0501_web2_orlikowskiwoerner-pdf/.

O'Reilly, T. What is Web 2.0: Design patterns and business models for the next generation of software, 2005. Acesso em: 27 dez, 2010. Disponível em: http://oreilly.com/web2/archive/what-is-web-20.html.

Oxford Dictionaries (OD). Accessed: 23 jun, 2011. Available in: http://oxforddictionaries.com/, 2011.

Pimentel, M., Gerosa, M. A., Fuks, H. Sistemas de comunicação para colaboração. In: Pimentel, M., Fuks, H. (Eds.), *Sistemas colaborativos*. Rio de Janeiro, Brazil: Elsevier, 2011, 375 pp.

Pires, R. P. Uma teoria dos processos de integração. *Revista Sociologia—Problemas e Práticas*, 30, 9–54, 1999.

Procópio, M. L. Cooperação e Organização: como uma idéia pode ajudar a entender a outra? In: *ENANPAD*, 30, 2006, Salvador, Brazil. Anais... Salvador, Brazil: XXX ENANPAD, 2006.

Ramaswamy, V., Gouillart, F. *The Power of Co-Creation: Build it with them to Boost Growth, Productivity, and Profits*. New York: Free Press, 2010.

Richardson, R. J. *Pesquisa Social: métodos e técnicas*, 3ª ed. São Paulo, Brazil: Atlas, 1999.

Sherman, R. R., Webb, R. B. Qualitative research in education: A focus. In: Sherman, R. R., Webb, R. B. (Eds.), *Qualitative Research in Education: Focus and Methods*. New York: Routledge Falmer, 1988, pp. 1–21.

Silva, M. *Sala de aula interativa*, 2 ed. Rio de Janeiro, Brazil: Quartet, 2001, 220 pp.

Stake, R. E. Case studies. In: Denzin, N. K., Lincoln, Y. S. (Eds.), *Handbook of Qualitative Research*. Thousand Oaks, CA: SAGE Publications, 1994, pp. 237–247.

Yin, R. K. *Estudo de caso: planejamento e métodos*, 4 ed. Porto Alegre, Brazil: Bookman, 2010.

Zwass, V. Series editor's introduction. In: Nunamaker, Jr. et al. (volume Eds.), *Collaboration Systems: Concept, Value and Use, Vol. 19. Advances in Management Information Systems*. New York: Sharpe, 2014, pp. ix–xii.

chapter seven

Enhancing online fashion retail
The quest for the perfect fit

Alessandra Vecchi, Fanke Peng,
Mouhannad Al-Sayegh, and Susan Hamilton

Contents

Abstract

This chapter broadly describes the e-Size project and presents the preliminary results of its first pilot test—an exploratory survey administered to a convenience sample of customers in an attempt to establish whether the integration of a size recommendation application into a menswear fashion retail website was successful by verifying the size recommendations made by the application and to assess the user experience of the application in order to determine its suitability for live user testing on the retailer's website. From the preliminary findings, it emerges that all participants found the size recommendation application easy to use. The majority of participants received the correct size recommendation from the application and would be willing to use the application due to its helpfulness in providing a size recommendation when shopping online; however, users' personal style and fit preference are important factors, irrespective of the size that fits them correctly. By integrating additional garment and fit information into the application, retailers can ensure that every user will be able to receive a tailored recommendation that meets both their size and personal style preferences.

Keywords: Online, Fashion retail, Size, Fit

7.1   Introduction

Drawing on our existing research, e-Size is a research project funded by the Economic and Social Research Council, exploring how online fashion retailers can utilize innovative technology to give consumers the ability to match their size and find the perfect fitting garment.

By assessing the implementation and deployment of novel yet existing software applications that capture body measurements and provide accurate garment size recommendations, in an online menswear retailer, the e-Size project aims to improve shopper satisfaction, increase fashion garments' online sales, and reduce product return rates.

The key objectives of the research are as follows: to further develop an existing software application aimed at producing accurate body measurements, in close collaboration with an online fashion retail partner; to enhance the retailers' customer satisfaction by improving the quality of their online shopping experience; to focus on user experience testing to contribute to the development of the user experience; to critically evaluate the opportunities and the challenges that are associated with the deployment and implementation of such novel software application for the retailer and for the broader fashion industry; and to contribute to the reduction of the economic and environmental impact associated with garment returns due to their poor fit.

More specifically, this project focuses on user experience testing: observing how customers interact with the size recommendation application; integrating feedback from customers into the sizing information provided by the application; providing guidance on improving the user experience of the application, and thereby the online shopping experience; and integrating feedback on the garment information into the retailer's operations.

Key to this are the quality of the measurement data from the retailer, overall user satisfaction with the online experience, the accuracy of the personal information provided by the user, and the effectiveness of the size recommendation application in matching body and garment measurements so that the consumer can find the best fitting clothing size. This chapter consists of four sections. Section 7.2 outlines the literature review, and Section 7.3 describes the methodology adopted. While Section 7.4 highlights the preliminary findings of the research, Section 7.5 illustrates the conclusion, the limitation of the application in its current state, and the directions for further research.

7.2   Online fashion retail: Benefits and challenges

Today, within the fashion industry, e-retail, conceived as a web presence alone (Ha and Stoel, 2012), is not sufficient for any high street retailer to operate or promote themselves. Doherty et al. (1999) suggested that Internet adoption might not be a viable strategy for all retailers, as the likelihood of an organization succeeding in their investment decision would be dependent upon the retailer's specific internal and environmental inhibitors and facilitators. More specifically, it was argued that only those retailers with an appropriate blend of technological and organizational capabilities and an appropriate product offering, which were operating in Internet-friendly marketplace, should contemplate Internet retailing, at least until the market and technology were more mature. Moreover, it was suggested that certain product categories were likely to have the greatest growth potential and opportunity to create competitive advantage: books, music, computers, and airline tickets were viewed as potential winners, while clothing and fashion goods were tipped as losers (De Figueiredo, 2000).

Traditionally, the term "channel" described the flow of a product from source to end user. This definition implies a passive unidirectional system whereby the manufacturer/producer marketed through a wholesaler or retailer to the consumer (Davies, 1993). The concept of the retailer as simply the final distributor has been supported by the emphasis on "buying decisions, operational concerns," and overall "product orientation" (Mulhern, 1997). However, recent developments in information technology are changing this orientation by enabling retailers to focus their marketing efforts on managing the customers more effectively (Mulhern, 1997). It is now widely recognized that the Internet's power, scope, and interactivity provide retailers with the potential to transform their customers' shopping experience (Evanschitzky et al., 2004) and, in doing so, strengthen their own competitive positions (Doherty and Ellis-Chadwick, 2009). The Internet's capacity to provide information, facilitate two-way communication with customers, collect market research data, promote goods and services, and ultimately support the online ordering of merchandise provides retailers with an extremely rich and flexible new channel (Basu and Muylle, 2003). In doing so, the Internet gives retailers a mechanism for broadening target markets, improving customer communications, extending product lines, improving cost efficiency, enhancing customer relationships, and delivering customized offers (Srinivasan et al., 2002). By and large, consumers have responded enthusiastically to these innovations (Soopramanien and Robertson, 2007), and online retail sales have grown significantly over the past 15 years and are predicted to continue rising into the future (Ho et al., 2007; McKinsey, 2013). This suggests a shift toward a bidirectional retailer/consumer relationship, in which more power accrues to the customer (Hagel, 1997). In evaluating the Internet's potential as a retail channel, a number of advantages, opportunities, and threats have been identified by the literature. The reported advantages are as follows:

Accessibility: Given the current rates of domestic personal computer (PC) uptake and the basic desire to communicate (Parker and Gulliford, 2006), the use of the Internet is forecasted to expand exponentially.

Direct communications: As an interactive channel for direct communication and data exchange (Verity, 1995), the Internet enables focused targeting and segmentation opportunities for retailers who can more closely monitor consumer behavior.

Cost savings: The Internet could ultimately replace the high street by satisfying all shopping needs online from home. This could benefit the retailer by substantial transaction cost savings (Ng et al., 1998).

New markets: It is predicted that retailers can gain additional sales, either to existing customers or through attracting new ones via a whole new global marketplace (Cronin, 1996). Furthermore, the new communication opportunities of the Internet provide the potential and easy access for brand positioning and diversification into new product areas (McWilliam et al., 1997).

There is a possibility to leapfrog stages of development since e-retail could facilitate retailers to shift from multichannel distribution to cross-channel distribution (McKinsey, 2013) by also implanting new business models, undertaking substantial rationalization of the existing operations (Vecchi and Brennan, 2009), and enabling the emergence of new collaborative practices across their supply chains (Vecchi and Brennan, 2009, 2011).

The anecdotal evidence provided by the experience of China is highly significant. According to McKinsey (2013), China has overnight become one of the most wired retail markets. Millions of customers can now log on and purchase a vast number of products that they could only dream of acquiring just a few years ago. McKinsey's analysis seems to suggest that 60% of online consumption is simply replacing off-line retailers but the remaining 40% is incremental consumption that would not have happened without e-retail. This is particularly the case outside China's biggest cities where brick-and-mortar retail remains undeveloped. E-retailing is beginning to fill the gap. In particular, Chinese consumers seem to buy more apparel and houseware than any of their counterparts (70% of the total online consumption), where astonishing growth has been achieved with very reasonable investments.

However, although the comparative advantages of using the Internet appear compelling, its potential as a retail channel will only be realized if a number of well-documented limitations are successfully addressed. For example, technical problems occur such as the complexity of the user interface's bandwidth restrictions and access connection speeds and security concerns (O'Brien, 2010). From a retailing perspective, the Internet also presents a number of problems. The use of the Internet is an elective activity whereby consumers require effort to access sites and products, and consequently planned purchasing may dominate overimpulse purchasing (McWilliam et al., 1997). The move from a physical to a virtual marketplace may require more complex product differentiation and positioning (Baty and Lee 1995; O'Brien, 2010). Fundamentally, Shi and Salesky (1994) warn that the value created by retailing on the Internet is unlikely to be additional but rather a redistribution of profitability from current retail channels.

According to McKinsey (2013), however, e-retail is not just a replacement of purchases that otherwise would have taken place off-line. It actually seems to spur incremental consumption especially where there is a demand for products that brick-and-mortar retailers have not yet managed to deliver. It appears that the true benefit of the Internet as a retail channel has to be traded off against these drawbacks. Additionally, these challenges are further exacerbated within the context of the fashion industry where the aforementioned challenges are coupled by some distinctive ones due to the intrinsic nature of fashion products. Fashion products are experiential by their nature (Kim and Martinez, 2012); thus, replicating the shopping fashion experience in the online environment poses additional challenges (O'Brien, 2010). High street retailers still find it challenging to communicate store atmosphere and excellent service via online communication (Ha and Stoel, 2012; Okonkwo, 2005). However, retailers that operate single and multiple channel strategies can provide a range of valuable benefits for customers while still maintaining heritage, luxury status, and service. This can be achieved by the innovative use of new technologies and digital tools such as 3D body scanning, style advice, codesign, and interactive screening, which enables an online retailer to equal or surpass that of the physical retail environment (Okonkwo, 2009; Ross, 2010). This is becoming a key strategy for the future viability of fashion high street retailers, as additional channels can provide additional income.

From the perspective of experiential web atmospherics in the fashion industry, there is a body of knowledge that examines such topic including Kurniawan (2000), Schenkman and Jonsson (2000), and Mahlke (2008). However, recently, Manganari et al. (2009) reviewed the subject in "Store atmosphere in web retailing." A conceptual model of consumer responses to the online store environment was tested and was compared with the physical store environment in terms of sensory perception, accuracy of product information, and social presence. From the findings, it emerges that all of these dimensions are equally important in the online store environment. This is in line with the findings from a recent study conducted by Ross on Savile Row's tailors where e-tailoring with the aid of a dedicated body scanner is a widespread practice (Ross, 2007, 2012). In particular for clothes that need to provide an exceptionally good fit, the anthropometric data generated by sizing systems such as body scanners can actually bridge the gap between "custom-made" and "mass-produced" (Apeagyeri and Otieno, 2006) and ultimately lead to a substantial growth of online sales (Ha and Stoel, 2012). Anthropometrics, the study of measuring the human body, has been considered by tailors and scientists for decades, but instead of using traditional methods of measurement, a good fit can now be achieved digitally. The big question for high street retailers is how accurately? This brief summary of the literature highlights the high level of interest in the commercial potential of the Internet as a distribution channel for the fashion industry and some likely implications for store-based retailers. A criticism of the literature is that much is based on speculation and informed comment as opposed to primary evidence. As such, there is the opportunity to conduct some valuable research by focusing upon fashion retailing on the Internet.

7.3   Methodology

From a preliminary survey of the applications commercially available, it emerged that there are various size and style recommendation/mapping services using a low-cost webcam, including *UPcload, Metail, Fits.me*, and *Poikos*. Some of these services require a minimum of two photographs—a front view and in profile. They also require detailed preparation regarding the calibration and segmentation of the captured image, thus making them difficult to use (Peng and Al-Sayegh, 2014). According to the technology acceptance model (TAM), there are two types of technology acceptance—perceived usefulness and perceived ease of use (Davis et al., 1989). Most of the size and style recommendation services fit into one category only, rather than combining both. In terms of ease of use, *Metail*, for example, uses a virtual try-on (VTO), where the users have control of their body shape, hairstyle, and skin tone. Among all of these services, the research team found that *UPcload* provides the most accurate measurement, with their entire measurement process taking an average of 20–30 min (Peng et al., 2013). *UPcload* was therefore deemed as the most suitable application to conduct some preliminary testing and hence was integrated into the retailer's website. During the initial stages of the e-Size project, the *UPcload* user experience was simplified, removing the need for a photograph of the user in order to extract the body measurements and instead requiring only three pieces of personal data: height, weight, and age. Two distinct garments were selected to test the application—a t-shirt and a hoodie—since *UPcload* size recommendations only work for upper body garments.

The research project has been jointly undertaken with an emerging online fashion retailer that only recently launched an online fashion retail platform to sell ethically sourced menswear, with a target market of style-conscious 18–40-year-old males The successful implementation and the deployment of the software application are particularly crucial for the online fashion retailer since it could enable them to build a distinctive business value proposition by also timely seizing substantial first-mover advantages within the industry. In particular, both the small size of the company and its early stage of its business development lend themselves to greater flexibility in the scope for the implementation and the deployment of an existing, albeit novel, software application. Such flexibility is crucial for the successful completion of the project, and the company's distinctive features make the chosen online fashion retailer the ideal industrial setting to engage with the user community. As such, there is the opportunity to conduct valuable research in relation to the implementation and the deployment of a novel application in the context of online fashion retail. This project is specifically framed around the user experience with the twofold aim to promote the elimination of waste through reduction of returns (highly significant for both its economic and environmental impact) and to increase customer satisfaction by addressing the balance between online and high street shopping experience within the digital era.

Drawing on our existing research (Delamore and Sweeney, 2010; Kontu and Vecchi, 2012; Peng et al., 2013; Vecchi et al., 2007, 2010), we specifically seek to assess the implementation and the deployment of a novel software application into e-retailer systems, to implement any corrective action that might prove to be necessary as well as make recommendations in relation to the application's implementation and deployment and its broader commercialization to the fashion industry at large and dissemination of the scientific results.

Primary data have been generated by means of an initial pilot test session aimed at assessing the successful integration of the sizing application into the retailer's website. Subsequently, the e-Size researchers conducted a pilot test at London College of Fashion to verify that *UPcload* had been successfully integrated into the retailer's website and that the user experience of the application was suitable for the customers of the retailer. The successful integration of the application would depend on the accuracy of the garment measurements from the retailer, along with the algorithm powering the size recommendation application. The suitability of the application would be determined by the accuracy of the size recommendation received by the user coupled by the ease of use of the application.

UPcload works by integrating a specific set of data for each garment into the application. It does not require precise measurement data for each garment; instead, it requires a "fit range," which is the range of body measurements that will fit a particular clothing size. For example, for the Rapanui t-shirt used for the pilot test, the size small has a chest measurement of 39.5 in. (Table 7.1), with a fit range of 34–36 in., meaning that it will fit someone whose chest measurement falls within that range.

Table 7.1 T-shirt garment data

Rapanui t-shirt	Small		Medium		Large		X large	
Product measurement	Item size	To fit	Item size	To fit	Item size	To fit	Item size	To fit
Chest circumference	39.5″	34–36″	41″	36–38″	43.5″	38–40″	45.5″	41–43″
Length	28″	/	29″	/	29.5″	/	30.5″	/
Waist	39″	33–35″	40″	35–37″	42.5″	37–39″	45″	40–42″
Hem circumference	39.5″	/	41″	/	43.5″	/	45.5″	/

/ = N.A (not applicable).

The garment data are normally supplied by the retailer or designer, but for the purposes of the e-Size pilot test session, the garments were manually measured. *UPcload* places importance on certain garment measurements, which for upper body garments are chest and waist measurements.

The fit range is determined by the "ease," which is the extra room the designer has added to the pattern of the garment during manufacture, to allow for comfortable movement. Depending on the style of the garment, the designer may add additional ease into the pattern in order to give a particular silhouette. For example, if a designer intends a garment to be closely fitted to the body, there will only be a minimal amount of ease; however for garments with a loose fitting shape, where the fabric hangs away from the contours of the body, additional ease will be added to the pattern. For both garments used for the pilot tests, an ease factor of 3–3.5 in. was used (Tables 7.1 and 7.2), which is a standard amount of ease for loose fitting garments.

Table 7.2 Hoodie garment data

Rapanui hoodie	Small		Medium		Large		X large	
Product measurement	Item size	To fit	Item size	To fit	Item size	To fit	Item size	To fit
Chest circumference	41.5″	36–38″	43.5″	38–40″	45″	40–42″	48″	43–45″
Length	28.5″	/	29″	/	29.5″	/	30.5″	/
Waist	39.5″	34–36″	41″	36–38″	43″	38–40″	45.5″	40–42″
Hem circumference	38.5″	/	39″	/	41.5″	/	42.5″	/

/ = N.A (not applicable).

The pilot test session captured the relevant data concerning five main areas of investigation. These mainly concerned each participant's body size, his online shopping habits, the accuracy of the size recommendations, the participants' overall satisfaction rating, and feedback on the application.

Eleven participants took part in the pilot test session on November 20, 2014. Participants were recruited via e-mail from the staff and student body of the London College of Fashion. Additional participants were recruited on the day of the session via a poster advertising the pilot test, located in the main foyer of the college. All participants were purposefully selected in the pilot test and were male, and an effort was made to recruit people with different body shapes and ages. Table 7.3 summarizes the distinctive features of the 11 participants in terms of their gender (all males), age, height, weight, and chest. These parameters were deemed as necessary to provide an accurate size recommendation for the two upper body garments that were tested in the pilot.

Each individual session lasted approximately 15 min. During the session, the researchers explained the test session and asked the participant questions on their online shopping habits. The researchers also asked the participants to confirm their height and weight, which were then manually measured by the researchers, along with their chest measurement, to verify the accuracy of their response, using weighing scales, a tape measure, and height measurement apparatus. This was done to establish the degree of awareness that the participants have of their body measurements, as this will determine the size that is recommended by the application.

Participants were given a tablet to access a dedicated webpage of the retailer's website, where they had to input their height, weight, and age

Table 7.3 Participants' distinctive features

User ID	Sex	Age	Height (cm)	Weight (kg)	Chest (cm)
1	M	39	185	90	95
2	M	19	178	68.2	91
3	M	34	183	93	97
4	M	21	161	55.4	84
5	M	21	173	57.3	83
6	M	42	179	87	98
7	M	48	182	75.6	95
8	M	25	186	69	86
9	M	33	187.5	76	99
10	M	27	177	80	95
11	M	31	169	76	99

into the *UPcload* application to get a size recommendation for two garments: a cotton t-shirt and a cotton hoodie. Both garments were available in the following sizes: small, medium, large, and extra large.

The *UPcload* application is launched by clicking the "size help" button located next to the size drop-down menu on each garments' webpage (Figure 7.1, step 1). When the application is launched, a pop-up screen appears, where users can enter their personal data (Figure 7.1, step 2). The user is then taken to a page where they are invited to select an image that offers the most accurate representation of their body shape (Figure 7.1, step 3). This is followed by the size recommendation page, where the user is shown the most suitable size, based on the designer's intended fit of the garment (Figure 7.1, step 4).

The participants then physically tried on the garment sizes that had been recommended to them by *UPcload*, to verify that the recommended size was accurate and fitted correctly. If the recommended garment did not fit, or if the participant indicated a style preference for a particular fit (e.g., a tight fit or a loose fit), then they tried on another size until they found one they were satisfied with.

After the user tests were completed, the participants were asked to answer questions on the size and fit of the recommended garments and to rate the application overall by using a five-point Likert Scale (with measures ranging from Strongly Disagree to Strongly Agree) for the following subjective measures:

- How willing would you be to provide personal information for use in a size recommendation application when shopping online?
- How willing would you be to use the application?
- How willing would you be to recommend the application to others?
- The application is helpful because of the size recommendations it provides for online shopping.

7.4   Findings and discussion

Participants answered a series of questions on their online shopping habits and the use of size recommendation applications. The majority of the participants that took part in the session shop online, either quarterly or monthly. Only a very small minority of the participants had previously used a similar application; however, all of them indicated that having an application that provided a size recommendation would be useful when shopping online.

The *UPcload* application relies on the user inputting their height, weight, and age, which the application processes to produce a size recommendation. In order to assess the extent to which the participants were aware of their own body measurements, they were manually measured.

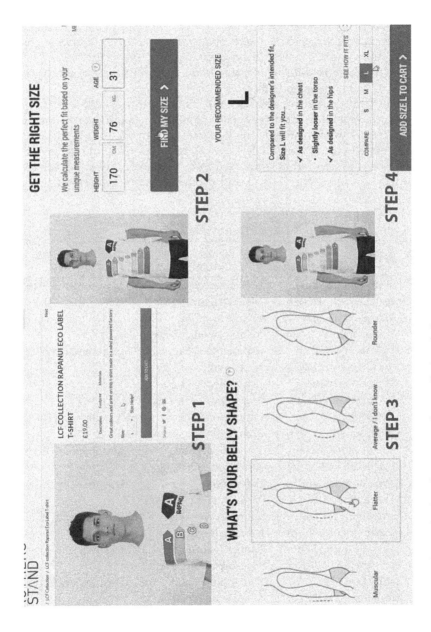

Figure 7.1 Using the *UPcloud* application on the retailer's website.

In addition to height and weight, the chest measurement was taken to give additional information on their body shape. The error margin between participants' own estimation of their height and weight and the manual measurement was an average of 0.74% for height and 2.96% for weight. This was not considered to be a significant discrepancy to present a constraint in the size recommendation process, and the participants' estimations of their body data were considered sufficiently accurate for the purposes of the test session (Table 7.4).

The t-shirt used for the test sessions was a cotton t-shirt, which was designed to have a loose fitting shape and hang away from the contours of the body. The t-shirt is available in sizes small (S), medium (M), large (L), and extra large (XL). Almost all (9 out of 11) of the participants received a correct size recommendation from the application and agreed that the recommended size fitted correctly, based on the designer's intended shape,

Table 7.4 Participants' size awareness

User ID	Height	Weight	Chest
1	Estimation: 185 cm Measurement: 185 cm	Estimation: 90 kg Measurement: 90 kg	Measurement: 95 cm
2	Estimation: 177 cm Measurement: 178 cm	Estimation: 64 kg Measurement: 68.2 kg	Measurement: 91 cm
3	Estimation: 185.5 cm Measurement: 183 cm	Estimation: 92 kg Measurement: 93 kg	Measurement: 97 cm
4	Estimation: 162 cm Measurement: 161 cm	Estimation: 55 kg Measurement: 55.4 kg	Measurement: 84 cm
5	Estimation: 170 cm Measurement: 173 cm	Estimation: 56 kg Measurement: 57.3 kg	Measurement: 83 cm
6	Estimation: 180 cm Measurement: 179 cm	Estimation: 85 kg Measurement: 87 kg	Measurement: 98 cm
7	Estimation: 181 cm Measurement: 182 cm	Estimation: 73 kg Measurement: 75.6 kg	Measurement: 95 cm
8	Estimation: 185 cm Measurement: 186 cm	Estimation: 67 kg Measurement: 69 kg	Measurement: 86 cm
9	Estimation: 187.5 cm Measurement 187.5 cm	Estimation: 76 kg Measurement: 76 kg	Measurement: 99 cm
10	Estimation 175 cm Measurement: 177 cm	Estimation: 70 kg Measurement: 80 kg	Measurement: 95 cm
11	Estimation: 171 cm Measurement: 169 cm	Estimation: 77 kg Measurement: 76 kg	Measurement: 99 cm

and felt comfortable; however, only a small minority (3 out of 11) of the participants would buy the size that was recommended to them. This is due to their fit preference differing from the way that the t-shirt is meant to be worn (with a loose fit), demonstrating that although the application generally provided a correct size recommendation based on the users' measurements, the style and shape of the garment is an important factor in deciding whether to make a purchase. The younger participants, in the 18–20 and 21–29 age ranges, on the whole preferred a loose fitting shape, as intended by the designer; however, the participants in the 30–39 and 40–49 age ranges generally preferred a more fitted look, where the garment either follows the body shape or skims the contours of the body. The figures show User #1 wearing the size that was recommended (Figure 7.2) and the size that they prefer (Figure 7.3), which is more fitted but could be considered too tight across the belly area. Due to the length of the garment, shorter users found that the size recommended to them was slightly

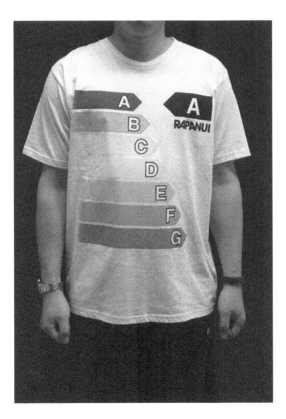

Figure 7.2 User 1—recommended size, XL.

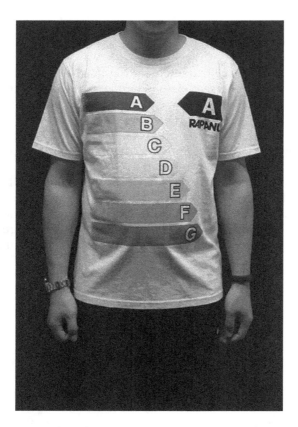

Figure 7.3 User 1—preferred size, L.

too long for their preference, which again is due to the loose fitting style of the t-shirt, and if it had been available in XS, they would have purchased that size, even if it meant it was tighter fitting in other parts of the body, for example, across the chest.

The hoodie used for the test sessions was a cotton hoodie and was also designed to have a loose fitting shape that hangs away from the contours of the body. The hoodie is available in sizes small (S), medium (M), large (L), and extra large (XL). The majority (8 out of 11) of participants received a correct size recommendation from the application and agreed that the recommended size fitted correctly, based on the designer's intended shape, and felt comfortable; however, only a minority (4 out of 11) of the participants would buy the size that was recommended to them. Yet again, this is due to their fit preference differing from the way that the hoodie is meant to be worn (with a loose fit); however, all users found that the sleeves of the garment were too long,

Figure 7.4 User 1—recommended size, XL.

which indicates an issue with the pattern and construction of the garment and had an influence on their decision to purchase the garment. Similar to the t-shirt, the younger participants preferred a looser fit, and the older participants preferred a tighter fit. The figures show User #1 wearing the XL size that was recommended (Figure 7.4) and the L size with a slim fit (Figure 7.5).

The two garments used for the pilot test were both loose fitting, and the results show that the shape and the style of the garment are important factors, as the customers' fit preference might be different from the designer fit. The pilot test demonstrated that the size recommendation application only works, and returns an accurate recommendation, if the garment data are accurate, the "fit ranges" are accurate, and the emphasis has been placed on the correct measurements. For garments outside of a standard fit, for example, loose fitting garments or particularly long garments, additional information needs to be given by the application, for example, *"If you prefer*

Figure 7.5 User 1—size L–slim fit.

a loose fit, try a size M" so that customers can make an informed decision on the correct size that fits their body and personal style preferences.

After testing the size recommendation application, participants were asked to state which opinion matched their view on four statements, using a five-point Likert Scale (where Strongly Agree = 5, Agree = 4, Neither Agree nor Disagree = 3, Disagree = 2, Strongly Disagree = 1). The response to the size recommendation application was generally positive. Nine out of 11 participants would be willing to use the size recommendation application when shopping online and 10 out of 11 participants would recommend the size recommendation application to their friends. Participants commented that using the application made them feel more confident about shopping online, as they often do not know what size to choose, and using the application enabled them to overcome their uncertainty about purchasing clothing online, particularly with a retailer they had not previously purchased from in the past (Figure 7.6).

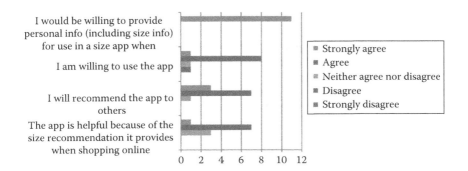

Figure 7.6 Participants' assessment of the application.

7.5 Conclusion, limitations, and directions for future research

Although we acknowledge the limitations in terms of generalizability of the findings that are inevitably associated with the adoption of a convenience sample, our findings provide an interesting "snapshot" of the fashion customers and their perceptions of the sizing technology and its promising potential.

As for the future development of the sizing application, from our findings it emerges that the sizing application is helpful because of the size recommendation for online shopping. While they also found that the application is accurate, they found the experience to be easy and straightforward. Nonetheless, there is room for improvement.

In particular, personal style and fit preference are important factors when shoppers are deciding what size to buy, irrespective of the size that fits them; however, the current version of the application does not take into account people's different preferences for fit. By incorporating styling information from the retailer and offering a recommendation that is based not only on body measurements but also on fit preferences, the size recommendation application can provide an additional level of service to customers and a more accurate size matching service.

This chapter provides only an overview of the preliminary results that ensued from the initial focus group that was conducted to assess the validity of the sizing application. Nonetheless, *UPcload* has been a success with the test users and the sizing recommendation results were satisfactory for all the participants. We have managed to offer a high level of tracking of body data for anonymous users and members in the database. The sizing application has the potential and capability to track how the body has changed over time, which could offer various different features to brands and retailers in the future. The main goal for *UPcload* is to enhance the shopping experience and reduce the confusion of sizing across different fashion brands thus ultimately reducing product returns due to poor fit. In order to create a wider appeal, it was important to keep the user in the same shopping environment and make the interaction between the e-commerce platform and *UPcload* transparent and simple, with minimal interruption to the user experience. This should boost the engagement and increase the confidence and satisfaction when shopping online.

Following the preliminary testing of the validity of *UPcload*, further funding for the e-Size project has been granted. This provides the research team the valuable opportunity to further develop the sizing application and test it with a wider range of customers for online shopping in close collaboration with a fashion retailer as explained in the methodology section. As such, the findings prove that there is therefore substantial opportunity and scope for the e-Size project in the context of online fashion retail.

References

Apeagyeri, P.R. and Otieno, R. Usability of pattern customising technology in the achievement and testing of fit for mass customization. *Journal of Fashion Marketing and Management*, 11(3), 349–365, 2006.

Basu, A. and Muylle, S. Online support for commerce processes by web retailers. *Decision Support Systems*, 34(4), 379–395, 2003.

Baty, J.B. and Lee, R.M. InterShop: Enhancing the vendor/customer dialectic in electronic shopping. *Journal of Management Information Systems*, 11(4), 9–3, Spring 1995.

Cronin, M.J. *Global Advantage on the Internet: From Corporate Connectivity to International Competitiveness*. New York: Van Nostrand Reinhold, 1996.

Davies, G. *Trade Marketing Strategy*. London, U.K.: Paul Chapman Publishing, 1993.

Davis, F.D., Bagozzi, R.P., and Warshaw, P.R. User acceptance of computer technology: A comparison of two theoretical models. *Management Science*, 35(8), 982–1003, 1989.

De Figueiredo, J.M. Finding sustainable profitability in electronic commerce. *Sloan Management Review*, 41, 41–52, 2000.

Delamore, P. and Sweeney, A. Everything in 3D. In *Proceedings of the first International Conference on 3D Bodyscanning Technologies*, Lugano, Switzerland, 2010.

Doherty, N.F. and Ellis-Chadwick, F.E. Exploring the drivers, scope and perceived success of ecommerce strategies in the UK retail sector. *European Journal of Marketing*, 43(9/10), 1246–1262, 2009.

Doherty, N.F., Ellis-Chadwick, F., and Hart, C.A. Cyber retailing in the UK: The potential of the internet as a retail channel. *International Journal of Retail & Distribution Management*, 27(1), 22–36, 1999.

Evanschitzky, H., Gopalkrishnan, R., Hesse, J., and Dieter, A. E-satisfaction: A reexamination. *Journal of Retailing*, 80, 239–247, 2004.

Ha, S. and Stoel, L. Online apparel retailing: Roles of e-shopping quality and experiential e-shopping motives. *Journal of Service Management*, 23(2), 197–215, 2012.

Hagel, J. *Net Gain: Expanding Markets through Virtual Communities.* Boston, MA: Harvard Business School Press, 1997.

Ho, S.C., Kauffman, R.J., and Liang, T.P. A growth theory perspective on B2C ecommerce growth in Europe: An exploratory study. *Electronic Commerce Research and Applications*, 6, 237–259, 2007.

Kim, S., and Martinez, B. Fashion consumer groups and online shopping at private sale sites. *International Journal of Consumer Studies*, 37(4), 367–372, 2013.

Kontu, H. and Vecchi, A. Social media and their use in fashion retail—Some illustrative evidence from luxury firms. In *Proceedings of the International Workshop on Luxury Retail, Operations and Supply Chain Management.* Polytechnic of Milan, Italy, December 4–5, 2012.

Kurniawan, S.H. Modelling online retailer customer preference and stickiness: A mediated structural equation model. In *Proceedings of fourth Pacific Asia Conference*, 2000. http://www.pacis-net.org/file/2000/238-252.pdf.

Mahlke, S. Visual aesthetics and the user experience. In *SchlossDagstuhl Seminar Proceedings 08292* urn:nbn:de:0030-drops-16240, 2008. http://drops.dagstuhl. de/opus/volltexte/2008/1624/pdf/08292.MahlkeSascha.Paper.1624.pdf.

Manganari, E., Slomkos, G., and Vrechopoulos. A store atmosphere in web retailing. *European Journal of Marketing*, 53(9–10), 1140–1153, 2009.

McKinsey. China's e-tail revolution: Online shopping as a catalyst for growth. Available at: http://www.mckinseychina.com/2013/03/21/chinas-e-tail-revolution/, 2013. Accessed October 5, 2015.

McWilliam, G., Hammond, K., and Diaz, A. Going places in Webtown: A new way of thinking about advertising on the web. *The Journal of Brand Management*, 4(4), 261–270, 1997.

Mulhern, F.J. Retail marketing: From distribution to integration. *International Journal of Research in Marketing*, 14, 103–124, 1997.

Ng, H., Pan, Y.J., and Wilson, T.D. Business use of the World Wide Web: A report on further investigations. Department of Information Studies University of Sheffield, U.K. Available at http://www.shef.ac.uk/~is/publications/infres/paper46.html, 1998. Accessed October 5, 2015.

O'Brien, H.L. The influence of hedonic and utilitarian motivations on user engagement: The case of online shopping experiences. *Interacting with Computers*, 22(5), 344–352, 2010.

Okonkwo, U. Sustaining the luxury brand on the internet. *Journal of Brand Management*, 16(2), 302–310, 2009.

Parker, D. and Gulliford, J. Information, logistics and retailing services. *Management Services*, 40(6), 18–20, 2006.

Peng, F. and Al-Sayegh, M. Personalised size recommendation for online fashion. In *Proceedings of the sixth International Conference on Mass Customization and Personalization in Central Europe* (MCP-CE 2014), Novi Sad, Serbia, September 24–26, 2014.

Peng, F., Delamore, P., and Sweeney, D. Digital innovation in fashion—How to 'Capture' the user experience in 3D body scanning. *International Journal of Industrial Engineering and Management (IJIEM)*, University of Novi Sad, 3(4), 2012, 233–240, 2013.

Ross, F. Refashioning London's bespoke and demi-bespoke tailors; new textiles, technology and design in contemporary menswear. *The Journal of the Textile Institute*, 98(3), 2007.

Ross, F. Leveraging niche fashion markets through mass-customisation, co-design, style advice and new technology: A study of gay aesthetics and website design. *The Journal of Fashion Practice,* Berg Publishers, 2(2), 175–197, 2010.

Schenkman, B.O.N. and Jonsson, F.U. Aesthetics and preferences of web pages. *Behaviour & Information Technology,* 19(5), 367–377, 2000.

Shi, C.S. and Salesky, A.M. Building "A Strategy for Electronic Home Shopping". *The McKinsey Quarterly,* 4, 1994.

Soopramanien, D.G.R. and Robertson, A. Adoption and usage of online shopping: An empirical analysis of the characteristics of 'buyers', 'browsers', and 'non-Internet shoppers. *Journal of Retailing and Consumer Services,* 14(1), 73–82, 2007.

Srinivasan, S., Anderson, R., and Kishore, P. Customer loyalty in e-commerce: An exploration of its antecedents and consequences. *Journal of Retailing,* 78(1), 41–50, 2002.

Vecchi, A. and Brennan, L. Supply chain innovation for short life products: A preventive assessment of RFID deployment and implementation. *Journal of International Business Innovation and Research,* 3(5), 535–554, 2009.

Vecchi, A. and Brennan, L. RFID supply chain implementation challenges for short life products. *International Journal of RF Technologies: Research and Applications,* 2(2), 117–134, 2011.

Vecchi, A., Brennan, L., and Theotokis, A. Customers' acceptance of new service technologies: The case of RFID. In *The Handbook on Business Information Systems,* Gunasekaran, A. and Sanduh, M. (Eds.). Singapore: World Scientific, 2010.

Vecchi, A., O'Riordain, S., and Brennan, L. The SMART project: Intelligent integration of supply chain processes and consumer services—A retail perspective. In *Proceedings of the Symposium on Production, Logistics, and International Operations (SIMPOI) at the Annual Conference of the Production and Operations Management Society (POMS),* Rio De Janeiro, Brazil, August 8–10, 2007.

Verity, J. The internet: How it will change the way you do business. *Business Week,* pp. 80–88, November 14, 1995.

Index